BETTER RELATIONSHIPS
HAPPIER LIVES

12 Keys to Getting There

T E R R Y   T U R N E R

BALBOA.
PRESS

A DIVISION OF HAY HOUSE

Balboa Press books may be ordered through booksellers or by contacting:

Balboa Press
A Division of Hay House
1663 Liberty Drive
Bloomington, IN 47403
www.balboapress.com
1 (877) 407-4847

Because of the dynamic nature of the Internet, any web addresses or links contained in this book may have changed since publication and may no longer be valid. The views expressed in this work are solely those of the author and do not necessarily reflect the views of the publisher, and the publisher hereby disclaims any responsibility for them.

The author of this book does not dispense medical advice or prescribe the use of any technique as a form of treatment for physical, emotional, or medical problems without the advice of a physician, either directly or indirectly. The intent of the author is only to offer information of a general nature to help you in your quest for emotional and spiritual well-being. In the event you use any of the information in this book for yourself, which is your constitutional right, the author and the publisher assume no responsibility for your actions.

Any people depicted in stock imagery provided by Thinkstock are models, and such images are being used for illustrative purposes only. Certain stock imagery © Thinkstock.

Print information available on the last page.

ISBN: 978-1-5043-4124-0 (sc)
ISBN: 978-1-5043-4126-4 (hc)
ISBN: 978-1-5043-4125-7 (e)

Library of Congress Control Number: 2015915565

Balboa Press rev. date: 10/16/2015

About the Author

Terry Turner teaches communication skills at Shasta College, where she specializes in courses on relationships skills as both a writer and a lecturer. Raised as a military brat, she traveled the globe as a young child and continued that traveling theme as an adult. After graduating in 1973 with her MA in speech communication education from the University of South Florida in Tampa, Florida, she taught at USF as an adjunct professor. Two years later came a move to Pensacola, where she taught at the University of West Florida. Relocating across the continent was the next big move. In Long Beach, California, she worked for McDonnell Douglas as a course designer, workshop presenter, writer, and trainer on a myriad of topics ranging from computer systems to coaching, and from human relations in the workplace to management skills. Her last move was to Northern California, where she has happily settled with her Sheltie, Alex, and has no current plans to move again—but stay tuned!

This book would never have happened without these people. I dedicate it to them:

To Heather Dian Smith, who told me, "Of course you can write a book."

To Ken, who was my first editor, and to Leimone and my family, who believed in me.

To Peggy, who helped me with the final edits.

And to all the other gifted teachers I have had, and continue to have, in the guise of my family, my friends, and my students. Thank you all more than I can express.

Acknowledgments

Keith Harkin, for telling the story of messing up the lyrics, so I know it can still be wonderful, even if we are not "perfect."

Brad Meltzer, who reminded me of something I had learned from my father: one person who cares enough can make a difference.

Howard Liebermann, who taught me about "push/push back."

Kenneth Blanchard, Jack Canfield, Albert Ellis, Louise Hay, Julia Wood, Marcia McGetrick West, Betty Evans, Kathleen Kistler, William Ury, and Roger Fisher, whose books, workshops, and information changed my life.

Some day, after we have mastered the winds,
the waves, the tides and gravity, we shall harness
the energies of love. Then, for the second time in the
history of the world, man will have discovered fire.

—Teilhard De Chardin

Contents

Foreword

Relationship, relationship, relationship! That is what a well-lived life is all about. And the underlying mechanism or tool that makes a relationship happen is communication. It is one of the most important life skills that human beings require, and the level of skill that we develop will determine how successful our overall lives are.

Terry Turner, my friend, colleague, and mentor, has written an excellent book that is easy to read and filled with a wealth of knowledge. She takes complex communication skills and breaks them down into manageable step-by-step tips. She has provided a clear overview of what it takes to become an effective communicator—from being mindful of what is being said to you to actively listening, critically analyzing your thinking regarding each interaction, and using that analysis to respond in a strategic manner that is win-win for both parties. She heightens the reader's awareness of the importance of empathy and respect when communicating. And she details why using pauses when conversing, reflecting back to the other person what is being said, and naming emotions can strengthen your relationships. Further, she outlines the value of remaining nonjudgmental and tactful in your encounters. Finally, she addresses the power of problem solving and the beauty of understanding body language and how it impacts our nonverbal communication. She carefully facilitates our learning experience, concluding with an explanation of how these skills lead to empowerment and a better quality of life.

As a therapist for the last twenty years, I have dedicated much time and effort to imparting the importance of communication. Sometimes I have been successful, and sometimes I haven't. It takes great talent to be able to educate a variety of learners. Terry Turner has that talent, and this book is evidence of that. Every reader, from high school through retirement, will benefit from this book. It is so easy to comprehend and resonates so well with our own personal experiences that each tip becomes unforgettable. This little book is an excellent addition to communication literature as well as a valuable lifelong learning tool.

—Becky Bogener, MSW, LCSW,
psychological counselor

How It All Started

It hit me first on 9/11. It was a tragic demonstration of how important our relationships are. Think back to those awful events of 9/11. The hundreds of people in the towers on the floors above where the jets had crashed. The forty-four people on Flight 93. They knew there was no escape for them. They were going to die. When these people knew they were going to die, what did they do?

You're right. They did not quickly make one last sale, read an inventory of their possessions, or review their bank balances. They called the people they loved to say, "I love you, and good-bye."

I saw this again last week. A plane traveling from Hawaii to Guam got into trouble and was forced to make an emergency landing. However, for a grueling few minutes, the passengers thought this was it. They were going to die. The news media interviewed a gentleman traveling with his wife, and he said that he and his wife held hands and told each other, "I love you, and good-bye."

I call this my *smacked in the face with the truth moment.* In spite of the fact that I teach relationship skills, I'd never fully realized this truth: the most important thing we have in our lives is our relationships.

So wouldn't it be nice to have a way to improve this most vital thing? Wouldn't it be wonderful to build, on a daily basis, the best relationships we can have?

Introduction

Imagine a room crammed full of students, all with blank faces. It was the middle of my "Theories of Communication" lecture. Lightning struck. If I didn't include *how-to* with the theories I was teaching, my lecture might be entertaining, but it would be pretty much useless to these young people. They deserved to know how to create great relationships.

So I started looking beyond the theories to find the *how-tos*. Happy couples—what did they do, and how did they do it? Angry, miserable people—what did they do that we could avoid? People who enjoyed their lives—what was different about the way they did things?

I've collected every bit of wisdom I could find and even figured out some cool tips and tools on my own.

For example, I noticed that the relationship skills modeled on TV and in the movies are for entertainment purposes and are usually *anti-relationships* skills. (I just made up that word. Works, though, doesn't it?) If you mimic them, the odds are good that you'll be mad and/or miserable most of your life.

Really? Yes.

Try watching your favorite sitcom, and pay attention to what gets the biggest laugh. Do you hear it? Insults like "I don't know why I married a loser like you" or sarcastic comments like "With that hair?" get the biggest laughs. That seems to be our normal way of talking to each other now. This type of language on TV gets high comedy ratings. In real life, it is hurtful. It is hard to spend your day getting smacked down by other people.

What are the results of this hurt, besides the obvious answers of anger, fights, taking revenge, and so on? What's our divorce rate, our suicide rate, our depression rate? Let's not even get into the homicide numbers. These are all high numbers. Hmmm. There seems to be a connection here, don't you think?

You might be saying, "Why do I need to improve my relationships? What's the benefit to me?" What I've observed as the result of people cleaning up their relationship habits is that they enjoy every day more, and people love being with them. Don't stress; I can prove it.

Think of someone you know who has absolutely lousy communication skills. You know who I mean— that person who barks and bites his or her way through every conversation. Even if he or she is the president of a multinational corporation, or just your grumpy coworker in the next cubicle at work, would you say that person is happy? Neither would I. Not only that, but who wants to be with people like that? No one I can think of. What are their marriages like? I think the phrase we are looking for is "they stink." Married forty years, and they hate each other.

Why live like that if there is an easy and viable alternative? Well, maybe it's not always easy, but I believe it is certainly worth the effort to learn these tools to help make your relationships better.

I included these *how-tos* in my lecture, and students have told me that these skills have changed their lives—better relationships equals happier lives. One student suggested I write the *how-tos* down in a book, but writing a book was scary to me. What moved me into putting words on the page was when she said, "Just write it like you're talking to us." So I did.

All the skills in this book work, assuming you're in a relationship with an emotionally functional person. If not, you need a different kind of book so you can smack that person in the head—no, of course not! That's just my cheeky self talking. Truly, though, there are fantastic books and therapists to assist you in dealing with dysfunctional people. Please seek them out if you are in a relationship that is painful or toxic.

Before we move forward, I'd like to repeat that learning these skills may not always be easy, but I believe it is certainly worth the effort. Remember that you must be willing to change before you'll put out the effort to do so—in other words, *you gotta wanna*. It's like losing weight. It may feel like the chocolate bars are calling my name, and so until I firmly incorporate my new, healthy eating habits, scarfing down chocolate bars and watching my waist expand will be a fact of life. But when I commit to change—when I find my *gotta wanna*—and eat the healthful alternatives, I achieve my vision of a trimmer and healthier body. The same is true in my relationships with other people. When I commit to communicating better—when I find my *gotta wanna*—my life becomes a happier one.

So here we go—twelve keys that will make your relationships better.

KEY ONE

Pay Attention

From your first word to the presentation you gave last week at work, you've been talking for a long time. Have you noticed, though, that you still have problems communicating?

Here's the issue: because we communicate so much and so often, we no longer pay attention. Our communication is all background to us. Ignoring this background or assuming that our communication is fine can backfire.

Think of it like turning on the garden hose to fill your child's wading pool or to water your garden. If you aren't paying attention and checking on the hose every so often, you end up with a soggy mess. Could this be happening to your relationships? Could you be putting good communication skills into the background?

I've discovered that I'm not the only one who puts important things into the background without realizing it. I need to pay attention, check in on myself and my relationships every so often, and use the skills I have learned.

Here's a drawing exercise to prove that once you mentally label something as background, you will not notice it, even if you see it a hundred times a day.

Exercise: You Mean My Watch Has Roman Numerals?

Choose something you see often, such as your watch, your cell phone screen, your driver's license, etc. Grab a pen and paper. (I'll wait here.) Without looking at that object, draw all the details you remember about it. Only take a minute or so on this—you're not creating an artistic masterpiece, just noting what you remember as being on the face of your watch, cell phone, etc.

For those of you who are like me and worry about making it perfect, I'd like to add that I've had my students do this exercise in my classes for quite a while. No one draws the items perfectly, so welcome to the club.

Once you are finished, compare your drawing with the object you chose.

Isn't it amazing? We all miss at least some of the details of the object we look at all the time. No matter how many times we stare at our watch or cell, there are details that are invisible to us because we have labeled them as background. My favorite example of this comes from when I used this exercise in class. One of the students, Mark, called out, "What? My watch has Roman numerals on it!" We all chuckled at his surprise.

I understood Mark's surprise. I've owned my watch for twelve years. As a teacher, I look at it hundreds of times a day. I've always assumed the "3" simply looked funny. I never examined it closely, because I had turned it into background. A clerk changed the battery last week. He commented on how convenient it was that my watch had the date instead of the number "3." I realized my error and chuckled at myself. We all miss the background.

Of course, being able to draw these specific things really doesn't matter in the grand scheme of life. I love how this activity makes the point for me though. If I've labeled it background, I just don't notice what's really there. I believe it's a survival thing—we are wired to ignore what we've labeled as background, or unimportant right now. Seeing the saber-toothed tiger charging me is more important than noticing the red clay paint used in the cave drawing beside me.

For most of us, our communication skills—the things we say and do that will strengthen or damage our relationships—have become complete background. That's the most common cause of problems that start in a friendship, family, or marriage. This means that we could be in what is (or could be) a wonderful relationship, yet there are things between us that are slipping or cracking or even fracturing beyond repair because we aren't paying attention. We've put our communication into the background. We don't realize that we need a communication tune-up.

How would you respond if a friend said to you, "My car's been running fine since I bought it. I don't need the 25,000 mile tune-up"? At this point, anyone who knows anything about car maintenance is mentally yelling, "Get the tune-up!"

It's a much better plan to catch a problem early, when it's smaller and easier to fix. This prevents serious problems that would leave us stranded on the side of the road. Our relationship skills, like our cars, need regular maintenance. Paying attention allows us to notice the signals that tell us it's time to tune up the relationship to help ensure health and longevity. We are more likely to enjoy our lives when we communicate better. Also, even with great skills, we will sometimes still mess up. The good news is that the mess-ups will be smaller. As I like to say, "At least I'll know when I've stuck my foot in my mouth and can do something about it right away."

I think this is especially important because of the *anti-relationship* skills I mentioned earlier. You know how you pick up words and phrases from the people you spend time with? And from TV shows you watch? Sometimes, we haven't even realized that we've started to model the smack-downs we've heard.

How does this apply to your life? First, pay attention to how you talk to others. What comes out of your mouth? Kind words or snippy words? What's your tone of voice? Harsh or soft? Next, start noticing how the people you know talk to each other. Are they commenting on what they like about each other? If so, yay! Or do you hear smack-down after smack-down? Unfortunately, more and more often, that's our normal. On the other hand, if we pay attention and make adjustments, we can build happier lives.

KEY TWO

Push/Push Back

Sometimes I wonder if our current cultural belief is that our words have no consequences. We often use cruel sarcasm or insults followed by a "just kidding" disclaimer. If someone calls you an obnoxious jerk and then says he was just kidding, what goes through your head? Let me guess. If you're like me, you start wondering if it's true.

We act like it doesn't matter what hurtful things we say—as long as we didn't mean to hurt the other person. But as the punch line of an old joke goes, "You can't get there from here." We can't get to a good relationship if we only communicate through the barbs of insults and backbiting. If we speak to each other that way, we generally end up angry.

Which leads me to the second key—push/push back. Or, *how to tick off your loved ones in nothing flat.* If you often communicate through criticism and insults, it is likely that people will attack back in one way or another. You push; they push back.

Here's a demonstration of it. You'll need to grab a partner—not literally, of course. This exercise is about pushing.

Exercise: The Game of Push/Push Back

➢ Ask your partner to raise his or her right hand as if to *high-five* you or swear an oath.

➢ Raise your right hand too. Place your right palm against your partner's right palm.

➢ Firmly push against your partner's palm for four to five seconds.

➢ Stop pushing.

What happens? As you push, your partner may let you push his or her hand back a little ways, but then, almost without exception, the other person resists. Your partner pushes back—without being told to do so. You can almost see it in your partner's face. He or she thinks, *Wait a minute. You can't push on me*, and starts to push back.

This is one key reason that good communication skills are crucial. If I attack another person with what I say or do, I am pushing. If I push with my words or actions, the other person will—let's say it together—*push back.*

If I use phrases like "You always," "What were you thinking?", "You never," and "That's really stupid," I am pushing. The result? The other person will find a way to push back. The walls go up; the person goes into defense mode and is ready to attack.

If you like playing push/push back, feel free to continue. Personally, I find it painful and exhausting.

On the other hand, if you want to change the push/push back dynamic, it helps to realize how you are pushing, in order to stop it.

When I'm hurt or angry and tempted to say something that won't get me an outcome I want to live with, knowing about push/push back helps me avoid that cycle of destruction.

Now that you know about push/push back, you can work to eliminate the types of comments that trigger the cycle: comments like "It's all your fault," "What were you thinking?", "What a dumb idea," and so on. Remember: these kinds of comments are a big old push—and the other person will push back. Then you've both jumped into the pool of hurt and anger. Is that really where you want to swim? Of course not. Neither do I. Everybody out of the pool!

Reduce Your "But"

(No, not the one you work on at the gym.)

One common way we push at things is with our *but*. Isn't that a great visual image? Hmm, come to think of it, we use more a side-of-the-hip push to shut that stubborn car door. Using a side-of-the-hip push or your real butt can solve a problem. Using the word *but* creates one. The word *but* means "delete whatever came before."

You now may be saying, "What on earth is she talking about?"

As soon as we hear the word *but* in a comment about us, we brace ourselves, believing that everything after it will be a verbal knife. Our walls go up, and before we even hear the rest of the sentence, we prepare for an attack.

As you read the following phrases, without knowing what comes next, can you feel yourself tense up?

"I love you, but ..."

"This was a good report, but ..."

"Your results came in, but ..."

"I'd like to spend more time with you, but ..."

"Our date was fun, but ..."

Using the word *but* after a statement or a compliment isn't effective. It's as if the person lifts us up and then smacks us down. A smack-down is a big ol' push. And if we are pushed, our instincts are to—yes—push back.

Can you ever say *but*? Yes, of course. The words *but* or *however* work very well in conversations on topics that are not comments about another person or his or her personality, appearance, or work.

Examples:

"I planned to fly, but I took the train instead."

"We want great marriages, but we aren't taught the skills we need to have them."

"I thought the prediction was for snow, but we didn't get any."

Please notice that in these examples I am not talking about another person or about someone's personality, appearance, or work. When talking about other people or their actions, we need to completely eliminate our *but*s.

How can you eliminate your *but*s? First, before speaking, substitute the word *and* for *but*—then listen to how it changes the sentence: "I love you, but the kitchen is a mess" becomes "I love you, and the kitchen is a mess."

Wow. As you hear "I love you, and the kitchen is a mess," you realize that these two things have nothing to do with each other. Love shouldn't be contingent on whether the kitchen is clean or not. Love is love. The kitchen is the kitchen. You can drop the first half and share it at another time when you are talking about your love.

If what you really want to address is the dirty dishes in the sink, if you are frustrated because it was your partner's turn to do the dishes before you cooked dinner, and the dishes are still in the sink, think about how to say it. Calling the kitchen a mess is a pretty judgmental statement; it becomes a big old push. Using the nonspecific word *mess*, what you say could easily be heard as, "Let me tell you what's wrong with you and how you do things."

Our goal is to move from being judgmental and pushing to being action-based and descriptive. No worries if you don't grasp action-based and descriptive completely. It's a part of key nine, and it gets its own section.

For now, though, ask yourself this question: what's wrong with the kitchen specifically? Dirty dishes that your partner agreed to put in the dishwasher before you started dinner.

Now that you've identified the specific problem, you can change your statement: "The kitchen is a mess," to a request: "Would you please put the dishes in the dishwasher so I can start dinner? Thanks."

Clarifying and being specific will work a whole lot better toward getting you the outcome you'd like to have.

How about another example?

A colleague comes to you for feedback on his latest report before he turns it in. You say, "This is a good report, but, wow, it needs to be clearer."

Your colleague has worked on this report for a while, and when he hears your comment, he might just want to give up and chuck it in the trash. Or he might feel like snapping back with, "I pulled an all-nighter on this, and all I get is criticism?"

Let's see what happens if you make the shift from *but* to *and*. "Your report is good, and it needs to be clearer." Not quite there yet. Not action-based and descriptive. What does *clearer* mean to you? Perhaps the report is missing something? Charts? More data? More clarifying text? Try including a specific statement: "Your report is good, and it needs a graph showing our monthly earnings for last year."

That is more helpful, and you are more likely to get the outcome you'd like to have.

In addition, for a subtle, wonderful shift, as Kenneth Blanchard wrote in *The One Minute Manager*, give the compliment at the end, so the compliment is the last thing they hear: "It needs a graph showing our monthly earnings for last year. That's all that's left. You've delivered a good report. You've made our department look great."

How is your colleague feeling as he walks away? Pretty darn good. How would you feel if you received this feedback? Same thing. And what is that final report going to look like? Yes, almost without exception—terrific.

Let's do one final example.

What if you're the boss at an auto shop and your new employee is having a problem keeping up the client files. You say, "Your customer service is great, but your filing is awful." What have you just done? Lifted her up—then smacked her down. This leaves her walking away with feelings of anger, grumbling about your poor treatment and how you don't appreciate how hard she works. She's not thinking about how to improve her filing, which is the outcome you wanted.

You know the drill by now: swap out the *but* for an *and*: "Your customer service is great, *and* your filing is poor." Better; the *but* is gone, yet you haven't clarified what specific change you want in terms of improved filing.

Nor have you told the person what exactly she is doing that makes her customer service so great.

The clarification and change could be: "I need to talk to you about your filing. It is important to file everything daily, so we can better serve our customers. And that's the only thing you need to work on, as your customer service is stellar. In fact, customers often tell me that your can-do attitude is what keeps them coming back. You are an asset to our team."

How will that filing be done? Daily, as you requested. Why? Because you gave the employee specifics on what she needs to do and told her what she is doing well.

Let's get personal for a moment. Imagine that you get to choose between two potential spouses.

The first spouse will talk to you like this: "I love you, but the kitchen is a mess." This type of spouse often includes comments like "You're so lazy. I do everything around here," just to make sure you get thoroughly smacked down.

The second spouse will talk to you like this: "The dishes on the counter need washing. Would you mind putting them in the dishwasher while I take the trash out?"

Emotionally healthy people have no hesitation. Spouse number two would be a lot nicer to live with. This works the same way with friends, which reminds me of questions I often ask myself: *Which kind of spouse or friend do I want to be? Which kind do I want to be in the future?* And I'll bet I'm not the only one who has realized that sometimes I've treated my best friends much more nicely than I've treated my spouse.

I can hear what you're thinking. Remembering to reduce your *but* and be descriptive is not easy to do. You're right. Any change in behavior takes work. I'll talk more about the process of how to learn a new skill in the conclusion. For right now, though, I promise it's not any harder than learning how to play a video game or drive a car—it may seem daunting at first, and, with practice, you get better. You just *gotta wanna*, start paying attention, and reduce your *but*.

Trust me; the results will be worth it.

KEY FOUR

Abandon Automatic Assumptions

(It's not always what you think.)

Once we've worked on our *buts*, we need to work on our automatic assumptions. What happens when we automatically assume something? The saying goes: If you assume, you make an *ass* out of *u* and *me*. Before we even open our mouths, the quickest way for us to mess up our relationships is to be an *ass* and make assumptions about other people. Been there, done that—and I'll bet I'm not alone on this one either.

First, let me clarify. Assumptions are not always a bad thing. Assumptions allow us to transfer knowledge from one situation to the next, which can help us predict what might happen. This is a sign of intelligence. If we have observed that using kindling makes a fire catch faster,

16

we can assume that kindling is a good fire-starter. The next time we make a fire, we can assume it's good to use kindling.

Where we get into trouble is when we don't realize that we may have different assumptions from the people we meet. We express our assumptions, expecting other people to agree. If we are with someone who has a different assumption, the situation could escalate into a fight about who is right. However, with just a little bit of information and understanding about each other's assumptions, that fight could be prevented.

One common assumption is "I know the one and only right way to do this." Unfortunately, this doesn't allow for the possibility that there may actually be hundreds of right ways to reach our goals.

For example, have you ever spent Thanksgiving at another family's house? Let me guess: they did things a little bit differently than your family does, and it felt wrong somehow. It was perfectly lovely, but it felt wrong. Yes, I've also had that experience. The other family did not follow the way we *assumed* the holiday should be celebrated—and of course ours is the one and only right way to celebrate.

Surprise! I know for sure that the right way to celebrate Thanksgiving was not inscribed on the original tablets handed down to Moses in the Sinai. In 1863, Abraham

Lincoln proclaimed our first official Thanksgiving holiday. He established the last Thursday in November as our national day of Thanksgiving. Yet we often assume that the right way to celebrate Thanksgiving, or any other holiday for that matter, was carved in stone at the bottom of those commandments Moses received.

While we are on the topic of assumptions around families, holidays, and marriage, let's talk about an interesting point: fairy tales lie.

Really? Yes. Check it out. Fill in the rest of this sentence:

They got married and they all lived _____.

No cue card is necessary. Everyone who has ever read a fairy tale knows what comes next—say it with me: happily ever after.

We have been programmed through story and song to assume that "getting married" automatically equals "happiness." I wish.

Instead, what really happens? We marry, and to our amazement, our partner has some different assumptions about how to handle all the details that go into making a marriage work. Marriage isn't the automatic happily ever after. For many newlywed couples, it's a serious wake-up call. They've come into the marriage believing the assumption that "my way to do things is the one-and-only right way." Yet a marriage includes such tasks as designing budgets, doing laundry, buying furniture, planning vacations, having babies (sometimes even surprise babies), raising the babies, unexpected illnesses, unexpected expenses—and even such minor details as which way to hang the toilet paper roll. So many of these issues have a hundred possible solutions—there is no one-and-only right way. Optimal ways, but no hard-and-fast, set-in-concrete, right way.

So, if we come into a marriage assuming it's an automatic magic wand to happiness, we're in trouble. We are working on these issues with a person who has a different set of assumptions about how things should be accomplished. We are in a relationship, and that requires learning conflict management and the art of negotiation—skills we will explore later. However, first and foremost, we have to learn how to manage our assumptions about what constitutes the *right way* to work on a marriage.

I'd like to expand on an example I first heard in a Kenneth Blanchard workshop. Imagine that you're sitting in a restaurant. You see a couple, newly in love. How are they acting? They are gazing into each other's eyes, smiling, nodding; each is waiting for the other to say and do yet another wonderful thing, and they are responding to each other with happy smiles and tender touches.

At another table sits a couple. They have been married thirty years. Gone is the misty-eyed, bated-breath phenomenon. It's been replaced by relative silence or a sporadic conversation that's no deeper than:

"How's your meat?"

"Fine. How's yours?"

"Fine."

So, I ask you: What happened? How did they get from sitting on the edges of their seats to talking about meat because they have nothing else to say to each other?

In my observation, the trigger is assumptions. Over the years, what has each partner been telling himself or herself about the other person? What has each believed about the other, based upon assumptions about what's right?

It seems to me that the process goes like this:

Newly in love: He's wonderful. She's wonderful. I love him. She's so great.

After dating for a while: I wish he'd change this one thing. I don't like this about her.

Moving into a long-term commitment: This is what a boyfriend/girlfriend is supposed to do. You need to do this and stop doing that for us to be happy.

Just married: These are my rules about what makes a good husband. These are my rules about what makes a good wife.

Long-time married: If only you would ... Why can't you ... That makes me crazy ... Don't do this ... You must do that ... I told you so!

That's how a couple gets from "on the edge of their seats" to "nothing to say to each other."

Over time, in a relationship, we shift our attention from what we like about our partners and narrow our focus to our assumptions about how they should be. Since our partners rarely cooperate by becoming the way we assume they should be, we give up talking to them. We don't like them very much. We have nothing to say. We are only going through the motions of conversation.

One of the greatest drivers of this process to the destruction of our happiness has been termed a *self-fulfilling prophecy*. Basically, it means this: if you believe something is true and you act as if it's true, it will eventually become true. We can help create happiness—or disaster—for ourselves by what we believe to be true and by how we act.

Imagine someone who is convinced that all she will ever be is a C student. In class, the teacher announces that there will be a free workshop given by a college counselor on how to effectively study for tests. Will that student, who believes that she can earn only a C, consider going to that workshop? Of course not; she firmly believes that she is a C student and nothing will change that. Believe it's true, act like it's true—and it becomes true.

On the other hand, a student who is convinced that she can improve her grades will go to that workshop and benefit from the new skills. Her grades will improve. Believe it's true, act like it's true—and it becomes true.

Self-fulfilling prophecies affect a marriage in just the same way. If I believe that my husband is trying to be a pain in the neck, I will look for examples of this. I will seek out things he says or does to prove that he is trying to be a pain in the neck. That will become my norm. I will then interact with him from that assumption, and I'll start pushing, which will lead him to push back, and, surprise, surprise, we both become pains in each other's necks. Believe it's true, act like it's true—and it becomes true.

On the other hand, if I believe that my husband is a wonderful person, that I chose well and I'm lucky to be married to him, I will look for examples that show how wonderful he is. Interacting from the assumption that he is wonderful gives me a completely different frame of engagement and a different set of assumptions about what he does. I treat him well, which increases the likelihood that he will treat me well (assuming, of course, that he is a functional person). Believe it's true, act like it's true—and it becomes true.

Becoming aware of what we believe about each other— our relationship assumptions—helps us use the power of a self-fulfilling prophecy in a positive way.

One final thought about assumptions: It's important to realize what we are telling ourselves about another person's assumptions. There are two possibilities we often use:

> **Possibility 1**: Keep your assumption intact and demand your version of the right way by thinking: *They make me crazy when they do it that way. Nobody celebrates Thanksgiving by eating ham instead of turkey.*

> **Possibility 2:** Abandon your assumption by thinking: *It really doesn't matter if we eat ham instead of turkey. What matters is that we are together to give thanks.*

Of course each of these will lead you to interact with the other person in a very different way, creating a completely different relationship.

Now for the big question: which kind of relationship do you want?

KEY FIVE

Embrace Your Empathy

If you're trying to have a great relationship and want to learn how to manage your assumptions, embrace your empathy.

I believe that empathy is the magic potion in a relationship. Empathy halts negative assumptions in their tracks. Empathy means that you mentally put yourself in the other person's place. You ask yourself, *How would I feel if that experience happened to me? What would I think? What would I do?*

Bingo! You have an understanding of what the other person is going through, and you are likely to be able to name the exact emotion that person is experiencing and understand why he or she is acting in a certain way.

The reason we ask ourselves the above questions as we learn to embrace our empathy is that we often automatically assume that everyone is having the same experience we are.

Here's a simple example to demonstrate how different our experiences can be:

In one of my workshops, I ask everyone to give a quick summary of what they did in the hour before they got here (using good taste, of course).

It's amazing the variety of different experiences people have had. The answers range across a broad spectrum: "I picked up a latte," "I missed the bus," "I dropped my child off at my ex-husband's for the weekend," "My sister is coming tomorrow for a surprise visit." Each of these participants brought a whole different attitude and set of experiences to that workshop. That's the way life works. Some were calm; some were stressed. Some were excited. Every person's daily experience is different. Because of this, we each perceive the exact same situation—in this case, arriving at the workshop—through a different lens, based on something as simple as what happened to us in the last hour.

Add the assumptions created in childhood to our daily life experiences and throw in our past and current relationships and—wow. We are all walking around with baggage carts full of automatic assumptions about how things work and how they are supposed to be. Many of us don't even realize it. That's why it's important to take the time to embrace our empathy by putting ourselves in another person's shoes.

Let me digress to help explain this point by telling you a little bit about my childhood. My father was a career Air Force officer and was one of the most empathetic men I've been lucky enough to know. With each of his new postings, we traveled the globe by air. Different time zones were something I understood early in life.

From the time I was two until I was almost six, we lived on an Air Force base in Saudi Arabia, where my father was the commanding officer. While there, we also took trips to Europe. And how did we reach Europe? By aircraft, of course. *Everyone travels by air* was my automatic assumption, based on my experience. It was the *truth*. And boy oh boy, do childhood assumptions become engrained in us, presenting a challenge when we are trying to put ourselves in another person's place.

Another one of the automatic assumptions I made while we were in Saudi Arabia was *Santa Claus comes in a helicopter.* For those of you who don't know, sending trucks out into the desert in Saudi Arabia without a compelling reason is ill-advised. Santa Claus's arrival didn't count as a compelling enough reason to risk losing a truck to a sand storm. My dad, with his empathy for the children and their disappointment if Santa Claus didn't show up on Christmas Eve, devised a truck-less solution. My dad gathered all the children on the base on one side of the hangar. On the other side of the hangar, Santa Claus got into a helicopter. The helicopter flew up and over the hangar—and there was Santa Claus! We were all beyond thrilled. It wasn't until I was in middle school that my dad revealed that Santa Claus had just come from the other side of the hangar.

Every year that we were stationed in Saudi Arabia, Santa Claus arrived in a helicopter. That's the way it was. That was the absolute truth. I'd seen it happen. Then we were transferred stateside. I started kindergarten, and those silly children tried to convince me of something about a sleigh. But I knew there was one and only one way for Santa to arrive: by helicopter. I was "right" and got into lots of arguments trying to prove it. (Okay, I confess. I was being a bit of the first part of the word *assume*.) Just between us, it was three years before I got on board with that silly sleigh idea.

As I mentioned, an assumption from my childhood was that to get anywhere, you travel by air, so of course everyone who travels has flown in a plane. Or as Walter Cronkite, the famous news anchor, would say, "And that's the way it is."

Now that you know a little bit about my background— having traveled by air for longer than I can remember—I want to share how empathy helps me battle the tendency to be an "ass" because of my assumptions. A few years ago, a dear friend in her seventies told me that she was about to fly to Las Vegas. This would be her first trip in a real plane! (The exclamation point was hers.) She was afraid of taking off, flying, landing. The whole thing. My brain stalled. My automatic assumption came into play. Flying was the only way to travel. Hasn't everyone flown since they were children?

Happily, my empathy kicked in right away. I mentally put myself in her place and imagined how I'd be feeling and what I'd be thinking, if I were a senior citizen and had never flown. I'd be scared too. Because of that empathy, I was able to understand and talk with her about her fears. Next, based on my years of flying, I reassured that her it was safe and she would have a great time. In fact, she did. This experience really got my attention about the power and hidden nature of our assumptions and how empathy can help us offer support.

One touching story of empathy overcoming assumptions was shared by a student of mine after my lecture on how the time in which we grow up automatically shapes our values. I used the Great Depression in the 1930s as my first example. I discussed the dire poverty. A loaf of bread cost a nickel, yet there were bread lines because people couldn't afford to buy bread. Jobs were few and far between, and there was a "make do with what we have" attitude. The student—let's call him Bill—exclaimed aloud, "Now I get it!"

When I asked him what it was he "got," he shared this story: Bill had gone to tell his grandfather exciting news. Bill had wanted a purebred dog for the longest time, and he'd been able to buy one for only $300. His grandfather went ballistic when he heard that Bill had spent $300 on a dog. Bill immediately became defensive and upset. Push/ push back—there they go.

But (and this is a good *but*) with his new information on what it was like to live through the Depression, Bill suddenly "got" why his grandfather reacted that way. The grandfather's reaction made perfect sense—a nickel could buy a loaf of bread, yet people were starving for lack of a nickel. Bill's empathy kicked in as he realized that spending $300 for a dog would be an impossible choice for the average person during the Great Depression. Once Bill had the context to understand his grandfather's assumptions, Bill was no longer angry. That afternoon, Bill went to visit his grandfather and had a healing conversation with him about the Great Depression. Bill's empathy and understanding mended their relationship.

What can we learn from all of this? When we put ourselves in others' shoes, when we take the time to think about what their day's been like, or we take the time to find out "where they are coming from," it's a whole lot⸱ easier to communicate.

The quote from the talented sculptor John M. Soderberg sums this key up for me. "Given empathy, brutality becomes impossible."

KEY SIX

We Choose Our Thoughts
(Master the pause.)

Most of us have never been taught this radical idea: we choose our thoughts and feelings.

In fact, most of us grow up believing the opposite. I know I did. We are taught that our behavior causes other people's feelings. We also are told that our feelings come as a reaction to what other people have just done. Guess what? That isn't true. Our feelings are created by what we think about what another person said or did. Our thoughts cause our feelings, and we choose what we think.

Have your eyes crossed yet? Mine sure did when I first learned this key. It's a novel concept. I wasn't sure I believed it was true. You may have that same first reaction. Most people do. Yet the truth is, to paraphrase

Eleanor Roosevelt, *no one can get you upset without your consent.*

Choosing the thoughts you want to have is a personally empowering tool. How can you choose your thoughts? The first step is to pay attention to what you think. Negative thoughts create negative feelings. Positive thoughts create—you guessed it—positive feelings.

Don't believe me? Try this thought experiment: Imagine that you are standing on the roof of a high-rise building. Walk to the edge of the roof. As you look down at the traffic below, you realize there isn't a guard rail between you and the thirty-story drop. For a second, did your stomach clench? Did your mouth go dry? Even though you are still safely in your chair, if you vividly imagined being on this rooftop, your body reacted to your thoughts about standing at the edge with no guard rail (yikes!).

The only person who can think inside your head is you. Let's examine this idea further. From the moment we take our first step, fall, and bump our knees, to our reaction when we are notified that we passed the Bar, the feelings inside of us are created by what we think. As a toddler, did you think, *Ouch, the tile hurts my knees* and start crying, or did you think, *Whoa, cool* and start rolling around? When you passed the Bar, did you think, *Great, I can start my practice,* or did you think *Oh crap, I have a mountain of debt?* Same experiences; different thoughts, different feelings.

Another thing to know is that our thoughts happen so fast that we often don't realize that we've even had them. Either negative or positive, our thoughts happen in an instant, or what I've coined as a new term in physics: *thought speed*. Too bad Einstein didn't write an equation about it.

When we recognize how quickly we think and how automatically we react to what another person says or does, we can change our interactions. It's not the person or event that causes our feelings. It's what we think about it—*Great, I can open my own practice* or *Oh crap, I have a mountain of debt*. The thought is what causes our feelings, whether they be happy or overwhelmed.

Albert Ellis, a psychologist, described the process. I've expanded on it thus: $\mathbf{E + T = F = R = O}$. This isn't another new physics equation but shorthand for:

> ➢ **Event:** An event occurs. Someone says or does something. Someone doesn't say or do something.
> ➢ **Thought:** We instantly think and create a reason as to why they did it or what it means.
> ➢ **Feelings:** From those instant thoughts, feelings emerge in our body. For example, our hands clench, our bellies tighten, steam comes out of our ears. Or we immediately relax, our hearts warm, and we go "ahhh."

➢ **Response:** The feelings (angry or happy, for example) determine what we decide to say or do to the other person: do we blow a gasket or pull the person into a big hug?

➢ **Outcome:** Whichever response we choose affects the relationship. Have we enhanced it or wounded it?

I'm betting that you want to enhance your relationships.

Now that we have talked about this process, let's talk about how to use it.

Think about your childhood for a moment. If you grew up with siblings, nod. If they teased you or you teased them, nod again. If you didn't have siblings, did you have friends whom you teased or who teased you? Do you feel the breeze now from all the heads nodding? It's pretty universal for children to tease each other. It's one of the ways that children communicate— a method that, we hope, most outgrow.

Now, the big question: Why do we tease our brothers, sisters, or friends? I've noticed that the answer is often some version of, "My teacher reprimanded me for not turning my homework in on time, so I'm going to tease my kid brother. When he gets all crazy, I think I'll feel better."

Fast-forward to adulthood. Some people, sadly, never outgrow the need to tease in an effort to make themselves feel better. You know the type. Their teasing has morphed into hurtful criticism. They hope that you will be a victim and let them continue to throw barbs at you. When you react as a victim, your reaction adds fuel to the fire. It's as if you are a row of cans lined up on a fence and they have handfuls of rocks to throw. When one of these people heaves the first rock, there's a loud ping and you fall over. With the next rock, you fall over even faster. With another rock comes another ping and another hard fall down. These people will continue to knock you down as long as you continue to stand on the fence and let them hit you with rocks.

Wouldn't it be great to stop that ping-and-fall cycle? I think so. It all comes down to choosing your thoughts so you can stop reacting automatically. When you consciously choose your thoughts, you can consciously choose your response. This is very empowering.

Let me give you some examples of how changing your thoughts affects the outcome.

Example 1:

Event: An event occurs. Someone says or does something. Someone doesn't say or do something.

For example, Mary and John have been dating for two years. Mary says to John, "I just don't think it's working for us anymore. I think we should start dating other people."

Thought: We instantly think and create a reason as to why they did it or what it means.

Possibility One: What could John think that would make him sad or angry? "She's the only one for me." "I could never love anyone else." "She's found somebody else."

Possibility Two: Have some fun now. What others kinds of thoughts could John be thinking that would make him happy? How about: "Well, we've both known it isn't working." "I'm glad she said something first so I don't have to be the bad guy." "I'll always care for her, even though we're just not a good fit."

Feelings: From those instant thoughts, feelings emerge in our body.

If John thinks negative thoughts, feelings of sadness or anger will occur. If he thinks positive thoughts, he will have lighter feelings.

Response: The feelings (angry or happy) determine what we decide to say or do to the other person.

With the first possibility, John attacks from his hurt and anger and says things he can never take back.

With possibility two, John agrees and expresses his appreciation that Mary had the courage to call it quits.

Outcome: Whichever response we choose affects the relationship. Have we enhanced it or wounded it?

With possibility one, the odds are good that they both will have wounded feelings that will linger for a while.

With possibility two, the odds are good that they will be able to remain friends.

By the above example, I don't mean to imply that we should take the end of a relationship lightly. I've only used this example to show the myriad of thoughts a person can have in reaction to a dramatic event, and how each of these different thoughts will create different feelings.

Example 2:

You're driving down the road with your wife. She chooses to give you a driving tip, saying, "The speed limit is posted forty-five here."

You immediately get angry and blurt out, "Don't you think I know how to drive?"

More than likely, this will lead to an argument—and the push/push back game. The trip becomes miserable. You rationalize that it's all her fault for criticizing how you drive.

Let's apply **E + T = F = R = O** to this situation.

The Event occurred—your wife gave you a driving tip.

Your automatic thought was, "She thinks I'm a lousy driver!"

Your response was anger because you believed she was criticizing you. However, it wasn't her driving tip itself that caused your anger. It was what automatically raced through your mind (at *thought speed*) that made you angry.

What if, when you got the driving tip from your wife, your automatic thought had been, "Oh, thank goodness. She remembered there's often a speed trap here."

See the difference? The Event was exactly the same. Your thoughts were different, so your feelings would be completely different. The two of you would reach your destination in harmony.

I wish I could promise that you will never have an angry thought. No such luck. We all have them. It's part of our human makeup. When we are in relationships, there are times when we feel angry. However, we get to choose how we react. The examples above are only to clarify how *what we think* determines *what we feel*.

So, you've had the angry thought; what comes next? Before you react from anger, mentally pause and examine the thought. Why do I say *mentally pause*? Because we think at light speed; we've had the thought before we even realize we've had it. We only notice *whomp! I'm angry!* If we take a second—the pause—and examine what caused our feeling, we can decide how we want to react. We recognize that we feel angry because of what we told ourselves about what the other person said or did. During that pause, we can realize what the internal trigger was from the thought—and we can choose an alternative thought that will lead to a more positive outcome.

When we stop and listen to our thoughts, we might notice that often when we get angry, a negative or self-deprecating thought is rolling around in our heads. When someone criticizes us, it can be an internal trigger for anger because, on some level, we worry that they might be right. We get angry because we doubt ourselves in some way. If we have no self-doubt about an issue, we don't get angry.

Imagine that yesterday you were at the doctor's office and the nurse measured you to the nano-inch with a fancy height-measuring machine. You now know exactly how tall you are. What would happen if I said to you that you are six inches shorter than the measurement? The odds are good that you wouldn't get angry, because who is mistaken here? I am. More than likely, your first thought will be, "Gee, she needs glasses for sure." No self-doubt; no anger.

Or: you are wearing pumpkin orange in honor of your in-laws' Thanksgiving tradition (you've adjusted your assumption about the one and only right way to celebrate

Thanksgiving: Well done!). What if I say, "I like that color of green you're wearing." Once again, do you get angry? No. Because the color of your clothes is factual—pumpkin orange—and there is no room for opinion or interpretation. We could get out a color chart and verify that it's orange, but why bother? Orange is orange, and green is green. You are wearing orange whether I recognize it or not.

On the other hand, what if someone throws a verbal rock at you and it lands in a spot where you have self-doubt? It's so easy to immediately go inside and grab hold of all that self-doubt. If you pause and recognize the self-doubt trigger, you can give yourself a moment to assess how you want to react.

So when you feel yourself getting angry, pause for a moment before you say or do anything. Quickly check your thoughts: What are you thinking? What are you angry about? Are you saying to yourself something like, *Oh, my gosh, I'm so stupid,* which leads to guilt and shame? Or are you saying, *That person is such a jerk,* which leads to anger? Now you can decide what thoughts you'd like to think instead. You might decide to think, *That's not like him,* or *He must be having a rough day.* These new thoughts will create different feelings and will lead to different reactions and a lot more positive outcomes. Of course, this can be challenging.

Once, I told my late husband that I must not be doing **E + T = F = R = O** correctly; I was still getting angry about stuff. Because he was known for being calm and serene, I wanted to know how he did it.

His reply? "I still get angry."

As I stood with my mouth open, thinking: *What? You do?* he continued, "Before I react, I ask myself if this person or situation is worth my time and energy. Usually, the answer is no, so I just shine them on and go about my day."

What a relief to hear. This was something I could do.

It's important to know that it is okay to get angry. We all do. It's part of being human. Just don't automatically react from that anger. Pause, examine your thoughts, change them, and change your feelings.

And yes, being human, you might need to go vent that anger later to a safe friend. I choose my dog. He's never repeated anything I've said.

If you can master the "pause" when someone throws a verbal rock at you, you have become like a field covered in fog—not a row of cans on a fence. No ping, no thud, so what's the point of throwing rocks at you? You have broken the push/push back cycle.

KEY SEVEN

Have to, Can't, and Should
Tossing Out Your Victim Words

In earlier chapters, we examined the importance of paying attention, pausing before we speak, and understanding that our thoughts create our feelings. There is another piece to this communication puzzle: watching the vocabulary we use. Words have power. Words create or destroy our perceptive filters. If you believe that man can never fly, you aren't going to help the Wright Brothers because you believe they are crazy. You stand in shock as their plane takes off.

There are three words that impact our perceptive filters in ways that can impede us from having the lives we want. These words are common. We use them all the time. Yet we don't realize that they are closing some of our perceptive filters. What are the words? *Have to. Can't. Should.*

Have To

The reigning queen is *have to*. Many of us walk around all day saying, "I *have to* do this." "I *have to* do that." Why do we feel so burdened? Here's the issue: When we use the phrase *have to,* we narrow our perceptive filters. There is only the one option in front of us; one thing that we *have to* do. We are trapped and often feel victimized by our circumstances.

Please say out loud, "I *have to* go to work." Did you feel weights on your shoulders and anchors on your feet? You've said, "I *have to*" and given yourself no other choice.

Now try this version. Say out loud, "I'm *choosing* to go to work." Can you feel the difference? The weights are gone. Your perceptive filters are more open, because your subconscious is thinking there are other options and you are choosing this one. It's amazing, isn't it? All you did was change one word, and you affected the perceptive filter.

You need to know that there is only one *have to*: We *have to* die. That's it. We haven't found a way around that one (well, except for science fiction heroes who get to be immortal from one movie to the next). Everything else is a choice. I didn't believe that either when I first learned it, so let's analyze it.

Before we start, let me clarify. In this *have-to* conversation, I'm referencing your daily chores, your job, requests by your family, that sort of thing.

Let's examine some arguments my students made when I first introduced them to the concept of *have to* versus *choose to*. They argued that there are a number of things beyond dying that we have to do, no matter what. They're Moses-and-stone-tablet things we talked about earlier.

One of my students argued, "We have to breathe."

No, you don't. If you cover your face so you can't get air, you will die—the one true *have to*—but you chose to cover your face. You can hold your breath for as long as you want, but a survival mechanism will kick in, and you will pass out and start breathing again. You don't *have to* breathe. You are choosing to breathe. In my opinion, breathing is a really good choice.

Another argument was about food. "We have to eat."

Do we? Yes, if we want to live. Our bodies require sustenance; therefore, eating is a solid choice, but it's still a choice.

Their final argument was about going to the bathroom. Any parent of a toddler being potty-trained knows the results if the little one doesn't choose to go potty in a timely manner. We can ask ourselves, beyond things like breathing, eating, and going potty, where else do we declare automatic *have-to*s?

When faced with the myriad details of our lives, we are programmed to believe our automatic assumption: we *have to* take care of those details.

But I ask you, do you really have to pull those weeds on Saturday? Do you really have to change the oil in your car? Do you have to study for a test or prepare the quarterly returns report? As I've said, none of these are real *have-tos*, even though they may be really good choices in your current situation.

I know that this is a brain jangle. What helps me to transform my automatic *have to* into a conscious choice is to ask myself this question: *Is there someone, somewhere who doesn't do this?* Yup. I'm betting there is.

For example, do I have to pay my taxes? I ask myself the question, *Are there people who don't?* Of course. So paying taxes is a choice, not a *have to*. I choose to pay my taxes because I have a healthy respect for the Internal Revenue Service and its ability to garnish my wages, fine me, or even send me to prison—the consequences if I do not choose to pay my taxes. My choice here is to pay. And because I prefer to be positive, I like to think of the good things, like firefighting, that my taxes help fund.

What about a young single mother in my class who argued, "I *have to* stay home with my children every night."

I asked her the question, "Does anyone leave their children home alone at night?"

Another student offered, "Yes! Last week a mother left her children home alone, and a fire started."

I said, "Therefore, the truth is you don't *have* to stay home with your children. The truth is you choose to stay home with your children, because you want your children to be safe."

I wish you could have seen her transformation as she realized that the deeper reason she stayed home was that she cared for her children so much that she *chose* to be with them in order to ensure their safety. So it was about *safety* not about a *have to*. She realized she wasn't stuck in *I have to stay home*. She could ask a responsible friend to swap babysitting. She moved out of the *have to* assumption and opened her perceptive filters to another option.

I asked the class for any other examples of their have-tos. A student insisted this was all well and good, but he had to drive his mother to the grocery store every Saturday. I asked if his mother owned a shotgun and waved it at him until he got in the car. After chuckling at the image, he realized that he was *choosing* to take his mother grocery shopping because if he didn't take her, the consequences were something he didn't like. I leave the consequences he mentioned to your imagination. He was able to enjoy his Saturdays a lot more and felt more empowered when he realized that this was his choice.

Can't

The second word that closes down our perceptive filters is *can't*. Unlike *have to*, there actually are some legitimate *can'ts*. You can't regain lost innocence. You can't unlearn how to ride a bike—you can forget, but you can't unlearn it.

What's the trouble with saying I *can't*? Remember the drawing activity in the first key? Remember Mark and the Roman numerals? As soon as you say I *can't*, you've placed all the possible alternatives into the background. They've become invisible to you, just like the Roman numerals were to Mark. A new possibility may be right in front of you, but you'll never see it.

Instead of *can't*, substitute what we've learned from *have-to*: "I choose not to."

Examples:

"I can't play the piano" will become "I choose not to play the piano."

"I can't find the time to clean my house" will become "I choose not to find the time to clean my house."

I know you're thinking, *How is this true?* Trust me; it is. Check out the piano example. If I gave up watching television and took lessons instead and I practiced in all my now-free time, would I be able to play the piano? Of course. The secret is simply lots of consistent practice. I'm not saying I have the talent to be a concert pianist, but I could get pretty good with all that practice. So, the truth is, I'm choosing not to play the piano.

How about finding the time to clean your place? Let me give you a scenario. You've been dating this incredibly wonderful woman for five months, you realize that she is the love of your life, and you want to ask her to marry you. Her parents are coming to town on Sunday to finally meet you, and they will be dropping by your place. What are you doing on Saturday? Choosing to find the time to clean because you want to make the best of impressions on her parents. It wasn't that you "couldn't find the time" to clean your place. Before, it just wasn't that important. You only needed to move it up your priority list to get it done.

A good motto to remember for this transformation process may sound like obscure advice from a guru in a science fiction movie. However, it is a solid motto to live by. "Do it, or don't, and then let it go." Choose to do it (e.g. clean your house), or choose not to do it (acknowledge that cleaning isn't high on your priority list), and stop worrying about whichever choice you've made.

Should

The final word that can close our perceptive filters is an interesting one: *should*. We've all said it a thousand times. "We should do this" or "We should do that." It seems like a harmless word, as in "I should exercise" or "I should change the oil in my car."

What's the problem? Exercising and changing the oil are both good things. Except, when you use the word *should* and take no action, all you've done is, well, say the phrase "should on yourself" three times really fast. What it sounds like is exactly what you've just done to yourself: dumped a load of manure on your own head.

The manure we've dumped is shame, guilt, and discouragement. You've created your own personal *push*. What will you do? *Push back* by not taking action. When we are "shoulding" on ourselves, more than likely, that oil change will get farther and farther from happening.

What can be more effective than dropping manure on your head? When you find yourself using a *should,* pause and examine the *should*. Ask yourself, how important is it, really? If it's important to you (leads to good health, makes your car last longer), you need to create an action plan for getting it done. "I *should* change the oil in my car" becomes "I have blocked out Saturday morning to get my oil changed." Or, if it's not that important to you right now (your car has another 500 miles to go before the oil change is needed), the *should* becomes "I need to remember to change the oil in my car at 6,000 miles" and you put it on the calendar.

So again, be like that science fiction guru and *do it, or don't, and then let it go.*

Here are two exercises to practice tossing out your victim words.

Exercise 1:

Get paper and pen and write down three *I have tos* you use in your life. Read it aloud. Notice the feelings in your body? Sit with them for a minute.

Now, rewrite the list. Substitute *I choose to* for each of the *I have tos*. Notice the feelings in your body? Have they've changed? Sit with them for a minute.

I'm guessing that, right about now, because you used the phrase *I choose to*, your brain is coming up with alternatives because you've realized your *I have tos are* really a choice.

Exercise 2:

Get another sheet of paper and write down three *I can'ts* you use in your life. Read it aloud. Notice the feelings in your body? Sit with them for a minute.

Now, rewrite the list. Substitute *I choose not to* for each *I can't*. Notice the feelings in your body? Have they've changed? Sit with them for a minute.

I'm guessing that, right about now, because you used the phrase *I choose to*, you've realized where on your priority list each of these three items lands. Do they move farther up, meaning that you will take the time now to create an action plan? Or do you simply need to let the idea go?

Remember: words have power. Words can create or destroy our perceptive filters. The more open our filters are, the more open we are to life. So I recommend putting a big red X through *have to, can't,* and *should* and making the word *choose* your new best friend.

KEY EIGHT

Paraphrase and Name That Emotion

(Oh, my gosh, you heard me.)

We take listening for granted. We assume that it's not that hard. We've been having conversations since we learned to talk. We just have to listen, then talk, then listen. The reality is, we're hearing, but we aren't always listening.

Have you ever played "telephone"? It's the game where one person starts the chain with a whispered comment. The comment is passed down the line, person by person. At the end of the line, either the original comment is garbled or there is no connection whatsoever to the original comment. What happened? Did everybody go deaf? No. It's really quite simple. We haven't been taught how to truly listen.

Let's talk about what listening means. When someone speaks, he or she is sending two messages. One is the content—thoughts and ideas. This is expressed through the actual words used: I had a really bad day. The second part is the emotion—what that person is feeling about what she's saying. This is expressed through nonverbal signals: her shoulders are slumped, and her voice sounds tired and discouraged.

To truly listen, you need to be aware of both parts of the message being sent. You need to recognize that there is both content and an emotion being expressed to you. To let the other person know that he or she has been heard, you respond to the dominant part of the message. For example, if the person's tone of voice is intense, the emotion is driving the communication. If you respond only to the content in this communication (I had a bad day) with an upbeat tone of voice and a question like "What did you do today?", you haven't truly listened to what the person is communicating. Ouch. Frustrating!

Don't believe how frustrating not being heard can be? Try these exercises:

Exercise 1: My Idea is Better

Grab your partner again to role-play the following dialogue: You play a person who has just won the lottery (yay!) and wants to book a dream vacation to France. Your partner plays your travel agent, who doesn't listen.

- ➤ You say, "I'd like to go to France and visit the vineyards."
- ➤ Your partner, the travel agent, responds by suggesting somewhere else: "How about the Fiji Islands?"
- ➤ You ask for France again.
- ➤ She offers Brazil next.
- ➤ Once more you say, "I want to go to France."
- ➤ She responds with a suggestion: Antarctica.

Continue this back-and-forth a few more times. Do you feel your frustration mount? It happens every time. Even though you know this is only an exercise, not being heard becomes very frustrating in about fifteen seconds. That's how powerfully we are affected by "nonlistening." Imagine what would happen if your friend had something really important to share and you became the travel agent, offering your opinion or other options instead of listening. You can tell how bad this nonlistening would be for any personal or work relationship.

Exercise 2: I'm Hanging on Your Every Word

Now role-play the following scenario: You again play the person who has just won the lottery, and you are ready to book a dream vacation to France. Your partner role-plays your travel agent. This time, she is a great listener—the best that she knows how to be. She hangs on your every word.

Isn't that a different experience for you? You find yourself getting excited, not frustrated. Let's analyze what happened. Because your travel agent listened to your content and your nonverbals, you felt heard. If, after this second exercise, I asked if you could recommend a travel agent, I'm betting you would recommend your partner. In fact, you might even want to take that travel agent with you on your vacation—all expenses paid—because there are so few good listeners. Finding one is like a forgotten $100 bill in an old wallet. Amazing joy.

Are there really so few good listeners? Consider this: If you had something important to share, how many people do you know who would really listen to you? Count them on your fingers.

The usual answer here is between "I don't know anybody" and "maybe five." If you're really lucky, or work in a career field like psychology or communication, you might have eight to ten. Now compare your number of good listeners to the number of people you know. The usual response is something like "I know a lot of people, and, wow! I only know two good listeners."

Isn't it amazing how few good listeners there are? Learning good listening skills can seem daunting, but they can be mastered with a little effort.

How do we become better listeners?

How to Really Listen

Becoming a good listener has two steps: *paraphrase* and *name the emotion.*

Paraphrasing means that you reply by restating the main ideas of what the other person has said but in your own words. Basically, you listen for the key ideas in his content and then reflect them back. If you do this as your first response, the other person will recognize that you have heard him. And if you misunderstood him, he can clarify what he meant.

The dialogue can continue because you have shown the other person that you have heard him without judgment. In response, he is more likely to listen to you rather than cut off the dialogue.

By paraphrasing, you aren't changing your opinion, only reflecting back the other person's. Through this back-and-forth, you may find points of agreement—or acknowledge that you simply agree to disagree.

Let's say you and your friend Tom are on opposite sides of whether peoples should be allowed to smoke in a restaurant.

If you don't paraphrase, the conversation could go like this:

Tom: There's nothing like an after-dinner cigarette and a cup of coffee. Everybody should have the right to smoke after they eat. I hate the ban on smoking in restaurants.

You: No, you're wrong. Smoking is bad for you and the people around you.

Tom: What, are you against the tobacco industry?

You: You're not thinking about the people who are allergic to cigarette smoke.

This argument is deteriorating into a game of push/push back, with each person trying to prove that he's right. Neither of you feels heard. Neither of you feels respected for your different opinion.

With your answer, Tom doesn't know that you heard his opinion, and he believes that you are only interested in bringing him to your side—and he's going to dig his heels in.

What have you accomplished, other than starting a fight with your friend? It's as if you said, "No, you're wrong. Let me tell you the right answer." This doesn't work very well unless you decided today was the day to pick a fight with Tom.

What does work? First, remain calm, and state in an even voice what you understand Tom's main points to be: he likes a cigarette with his coffee, and he hates the ban on smoking in a restaurant.

If you do paraphrase, your dialogue could go like this:

Tom: There's nothing like an after-dinner cigarette and a cup of coffee. Everybody should have the right to smoke after they eat. I hate the ban on smoking in restaurants.

You: You believe that smokers should be allowed to smoke in restaurants, and you enjoy it. (Remember: stay calm, and simply state this.)

At this point, Tom might rethink his position and reply, "Well, not everywhere, but at least there should be smoking areas in every restaurant for those of us who enjoy it."

If he clarifies or changes his statements like this, you once again summarize or paraphrase until he indicates agreement that those were his main ideas. When you nail the paraphrase with someone, watch his head. Almost without exception, the other person will nod, indicating that that is exactly what he was saying; he feels heard. I have yet to see an exception to the nodding.

Now, after Tom's nod, it's your turn to express your opinion. At this point, I encourage you to avoid saying something like "I disagree" because this can imply "You're wrong, and I'm not listening." Instead, I recommend using responses like "I see it differently," "I have a concern with that," or "I'm worried about one aspect of that." You get the idea.

Your response could go like this:

You say, "I want to share my concern about smoking in restaurants. Many people are allergic to cigarette smoke, and it triggers an asthmatic attack. What are some options we could consider that would allow both people's needs to be met?"

Now, Tom may never change his mind, just as happens on any subject. He may challenge you on your concern. Again, paraphrase what he has said, and then share your concern again. My guess is, if you do this, you and Tom may find points of agreement—or you may "agree to disagree."

With your good listening skills, however, you have avoided an argument, learned more about Tom, and given him the message that you believe that what he has to say is worth listening to, whether you agree with his viewpoint or not. This positive dialogue will make future problem solving between you more successful.

To summarize: When you paraphrase, look for the main ideas in what the person just told you and before you give your opinion, recap or paraphrase his main ideas in your own words. Don't repeat what he said word for word. Remember how mad that made you as a child, when your brother or sister would do that? You'd say something, and they would repeat every word that came out of your mouth. Don't do that. Adults hate it too.

Name the Emotion: Putting Your Empathy into Action

In key five, we explored the importance of empathy. As I said in that section, empathy is a magic potion in a relationship. When a person feels your empathy, she feels heard—it's like you've just given her a verbal hug. And after a bad day, who doesn't enjoy a good hug?

How does this work? It's all about the second part of the message: the emotion being expressed to you. Humans want to share what they are feeling. They can talk about emotions—saying "I love you" or "I'm happy"—but generally, humans express emotions through their tone of voice and body language.

When someone who is talking to you is displaying a strong emotion, you will notice it in her voice and body. If she is angry, her voice may be louder than usual. If she is worried, her shoulders might be hunched. The emotion is like a bucket of water she is holding. If you ignore the emotion and quickly offer her a solution, it's as if you've poured more water into the bucket. What happens? The bucket overflows. However, if you name the emotion, you are helping her to empty the bucket. You've helped her do this by showing your empathy.

It's wonderfully simple to show your empathy. All you have to do is name the emotion that the other person is communicating with her voice, body, or words. If your partner comes home from work visibly upset about how the print shop didn't deliver a report that's due, you could respond with, "Ah, honey. That is so frustrating."

Sometimes we are encouraged to ask another person if she is upset. I believe this can work if there is no discernable emotion being communicated by the person's voice or body. However, if she is visibly angry, asking if she is upset won't show your feelings of empathy—and the other person won't feel heard.

For example, if your partner meets you after work and says in a loud, tight tone of voice, "If I have to deal with that print shop one more time, I may lose it," and you respond with, "Are you upset?" your partner won't feel heard. You've asked a question about her feelings rather than acknowledging that she is obviously upset by naming the emotion.

Asking a person who is very upset how she is feeling is a great way to move that person from upset to enraged. In essence, you've told her that she's not worth paying attention to. Unfortunately, you might now become the target for all the rage she has stored up over the day because people *want* to be heard. Remember the lottery winner and the travel agent?

As you become more comfortable with the process of naming the emotion, be aware that repeating the same word for the emotion over and over can be just as irritating to the other person as you not recognizing the emotion. Don't say, "That's frustrating," then, "That's frustrating too," and add, "And that's also frustrating."

The other person will feel mocked rather than heard. You can vary your naming of this emotion by using frustrating, irritating, annoying, aggravating. Or, you can use the simple technique one of my students said he used when his friends were upset about something. When I asked him to share it with us, he said in a surprisingly deep voice, "That sucks." His friends all felt heard by that simple phrase, and they knew that he truly cared. And that's empathy—it's that simple.

Speaking of voices going deep, here's something else to pay attention to as you name the emotion. Drop your voice at the end of the sentence. Don't believe the difference it makes? Try this:

In an even voice, read out loud:

I'm wearing pumpkin orange to Thanksgiving dinner.

Now, reread it, raising your voice on the word *dinner*:

I'm wearing pumpkin orange to Thanksgiving dinner.

See the difference? You've changed a simple statement into a question. Depending upon how high your voice went, the statement could be viewed as combative rather than a simple declaration of what clothes you are going to wear.

In English, when our voices go up at the end of a sentence, it's a signal that we've just asked a question. Remember: we want to name the emotion we perceive (in our example, frustration), not ask whether the person is upset.

When you are trying to name the emotion, go for it. Name it to the best of your ability.

I've discovered that if I hit the same intensity of emotion, even if I've named the wrong emotion, the person will usually clarify which emotion he or she is feeling. The conversation keeps flowing as you help your friend empty the bucket. It happens like this:

Partner: I can't believe I forgot and bought Linda a café latte!

You: How annoying!

Partner: No, I wasn't annoyed. I was actually embarrassed. As I gave it to her, I remembered too late that she only drinks tea.

You: Oh, wow, that would be embarrassing.

And on the conversation goes, because your partner can tell you care about what's happening in her life.

What do you do when your brain goes blank and you can't come up with the name of an emotion? Guess what? Humans have a wide range of responses beyond words. You can make a sound, such as "uh-huh" or "mm-hmm." Whatever noise you choose, make sure it comes from your heart. This will tell the other person that you are listening, and your heartfelt tone tells him that he has been heard.

I also recommend *not* responding with, "I understand how you're feeling." A frequent response to that is, "No, you don't."

Be sure to allow the person enough time to vent and fully empty his or her bucket before moving to problem solving, if that is needed. How to do the problem solving is its own key, which I'll cover later.

I want to share four cautions that I've learned the hard way about showing empathy.

Four Cautions

> ➤ As another person is venting feelings, don't agree with negative judgments about another person. What do you do? Stick to naming the emotion.
> ➤ If the emotion being communicated is one that the person might not be proud of (greed, jealousy), consider using a sound instead, as discussed earlier.
> ➤ Refrain from giving advice. Instead, once the person has finished venting, help him examine the options and choices, and let him make his own decisions.
> ➤ Watch your nonverbal cues. If you are saying, "How frustrating," but you keep glancing out the window, the person will definitely not feel heard.

To close out this key, let's review for a moment how to be a good listener. To show someone that you've heard him or her, address both parts of the message: the content and the feeling. Depending upon which part of the message is dominant, either paraphrase the person's words or name the emotion you perceive he or she is sharing.

That's all there is to it. Now you're doing more than just using your two ears to listen; you're using what's between them. You've graduated. You've been added to the finger-counting roster of good listeners. Well Done!

Strive for Tact

(Butter won't melt in my mouth.)

As you've noticed by now, some words build a relationship, while others are destructive and should be avoided. This leads us to the next layer in the process of good communication: tact. Using tact means asking for what you want or need without pushing on the other person. It means using descriptive or action-based, rather than judgmental, words. At its roots, tact is saying something in a way that is comfortable for the other person to hear.

I recommend these four steps to using tact in your communication:

- ➢ **Do your internal personal work.**
- ➢ **Avoid using judgmental words.**
- ➢ **Be descriptive.**
- ➢ **Choose being kind over being right.**

Internal Personal Work

People give out what they have inside. Those filled with criticism give out criticism. Those filled with happiness share that. If your internal personal work includes appreciating what's right about you, you have "appreciation" to share with others. Listen to how you talk to yourself: What words do you use to describe your approach the world? Do you berate yourself or compliment yourself? Next, notice what you choose to focus on in other people.

Many of us have been conditioned to believe that we are lacking something in personality, character, or skills. We have been taught to always strive for perfection and to blame ourselves when we fall short. One of the most profound ideas I learned from Louise Hay and Jack Canfield is to say to yourself, *I am enough.* They didn't have us say, *I am perfect.*

We all have areas where we need to improve; I've shared some of my own in this book. The idea, however, is really simple. If we let ourselves be "enough" as our core belief, we will value ourselves. That makes it a lot easier to be kinder to ourselves—and to others. We give out what we have inside.

Give it a try. Say it a few times: *I am enough.* How does it feel? Uncomfortable? Wonderful? A relief? It's powerful in what it brings up, isn't it? Perhaps a sense of empowerment? Perhaps unresolved feelings from our past?

Once you know what garbage thoughts you harbor, you can begin to clean your mental house. If the garbage thoughts seem too big, seek out a therapist who can help you resolve them.

Saying *I am enough* is an important message to give yourself daily. You are telling yourself that you have something of value to contribute to your friendships, marriage, workplace, etc. Saying *I am enough* isn't about claiming perfection. No one is perfect. Having perfection in all things as your goal can lead to stress in you and those around you. A better goal would be excellence in all things—and accepting that some days, all we can achieve is "good enough for right now." Saying *I am enough* starts you on a foundation of "being okay" while still acknowledging your efforts toward excellence.

When we live with the motto *I am enough*, we are accepting ourselves for who we are, warts and all.

Here's a personal example that explains what I mean:

Since I thought my communication skills weren't perfect, I started and stopped writing this manuscript for years. Even though I'd learned *I am enough,* I kept thinking, *How can I write a book on something I'm not perfect at?* I had to wait until I was *perfect.* I put the manuscript away yet again to watch an interview by Keith Harkin, a singer and songwriter for the group "Celtic Thunder."

He is an amazing and talented man. The reporter asked if he ever got nervous on stage. He had, during his solo of *Mountains of Mourne*, a four-minute song. He'd known it since childhood. When he opened his mouth to sing, he completely blanked on the lyrics. Nothing was there. He knew he had to fill the next four minutes of the show, so, experienced performer that he was, he just made up lyrics with as much passion as he could muster.

When the interviewer asked him how he felt, Keith said, "Those four minutes were absolutely horrifying. I made up lyrics in front of 4,000 people, yet when the song ended and the crowd cheered, I realized, nobody's perfect. We all make mistakes, and it's our mistakes that can still sometimes make something beautiful. So no one's perfect."

Thank you, Keith, for the reminder that we don't have to be perfect; we just have to try.

I got out my manuscript again.

If you are comfortable in your own skin, you can relate in a loving manner to your friends and family. They are enough too.

Avoid Using Judgmental Words

To achieve the outcomes that I am describing, it's necessary to move from judging and pushing another person to describing his or her actions without judgment.

What do I mean by judgment? A judgment is your opinion or analysis of another person's actions. You may think that you are being factual, and you might even base your judgment in fact, but a judgment is a big ol' push. When you push on others, they'll do what? Yes. Push back. (100 percent on the pop quiz for you today.) So stay out of push/push back.

Remember the kitchen example? Saying that the kitchen is a mess is a judgment. If you are more specific and mention the dirty dishes that your partner agreed to put in the dishwasher before you started dinner, you are describing an action. When you are specific like this, people are more willing to listen to your requests, and you are more likely to achieve the outcomes you want. You'll notice that, as you begin to practice being descriptive, it becomes easier.

Be Descriptive

Being judgmental is our cultural norm. You might believe that you are asking for an action, but the person you are talking to might not understand your request that way.

71

When you're going to ask someone to do something or to stop doing something, as you frame your request, ask yourself, *If I asked ten people to act this out, could they do it without thinking about it? Would it look pretty much identical?* If the answer is no, what you are requesting is not an action or a description; it may well be a judgment. If the answer is yes, you get another 100 percent on the pop quiz.

How do we determine whether a word is descriptive or judgmental? Let me share an exercise I do in class. I ask the students for an example of this concept. Often the example given is that someone is "being cold" to the speaker.

The rest of the exercise goes like this:

Me: What's the description in that sentence?

Student: He's being cold to me.

Me: Precisely, what is he doing?

Student: He's being cold to me.

Me: Okay. Act out "being cold to me."

Student: Uh … I'm not sure how.

When you have that "uh, I'm not sure how," moment, that's the signal. What you've said is not an action; it's your opinion, your judgment. How do you know this? There are probably 8,000 actions that could fall in the category of "being cold to me." The other person isn't sure which one of those 8,000 specific actions you are referring to. So the response is often confusion.

If the other person doesn't know precisely what's bugging you, how will he know precisely what to change? Also, the statement itself, is a push; therefore, he will push back.

The conversation might go like this:

You: You're being cold to me.

Partner: No, I'm not.

You: Yes, you are.

Stop right there. Before you speak, think about what action your partner did that you interpreted as cold. Then frame it so it will be comfortable for her to hear (using tact). "I went to hug you, and you didn't hug me back." This is a description of her behavior.

Notice that, if you asked someone to act out that scenario, most people could easily replicate it. That is a description, not a judgment.

The next piece, of course, is to consider what action you would like the other person to do instead and add that into your statement: "I went to hug you, and you didn't hug me back. I would love a hug from you."

This is quite different from how we often talk to each other, and clear communication like this can lead to a better outcome and a better relationship.

When you request a new action or behavior from your partner, remember to thank her when she makes the change. It's too easy to think, *that takes care of that* and not mention it again. It took effort and caring on your partner's part—effort that deserves to be acknowledged in a descriptive way: "It was so nice to walk into the kitchen and see that all the dishes were done. Thanks."

One final thought for this idea: Avoid absolutes. This means to avoid using words like *never* or *always*. Not only will you get a push back, but you may also feel like you are trapped in Vaudeville routine. For example:

You: You never feed the dog.
Partner: Oh, yes I do! I fed him last week.

Ba-da-bing—and off you both go down a sidetrack instead of talking about feeding the dog.

A more descriptive question could be: "Has the dog been fed today?" A descriptive statement could be: "I'm counting on you to feed the dog today."

The more specific you can be, the better the likely outcome. The more you use tact in your descriptions, the more other people will understand what you want or need, which improves the odds that they will consider making the requested changes.

Choose Being Kind over Being Right

As you've read this book, I suspect that you've begun to notice on TV, at work, and maybe at home, some examples of what I've mentioned about how we treat each other (unless you're pulling an all-nighter and reading this book cover to cover).

Our normal interactions are often the smack-downs that pass as communication. Maybe you've realized that you've been engaging in proving you know the one-and-only way to do something or playing push/push back. If this is true, no worries. We all do this from time to time. Remember: the trick is that you *gotta wanna* to make the change.

Recognize that you are acting a certain way. Then choose a different way. Sure, we all make mistakes and have flaws. But why not lift each other up emotionally every chance we get? Why not be kind rather than insisting that we are right?

Here's an example:

You and your spouse work on different sides of town, so you drive separate cars to work. One morning, you notice that your spouse's right front tire looks low. You mention it. He says, "Yeah, I'll put some air in it today."

The next morning, the tire is still low. You mention it again, with, "Honey, that tire is still low. Did you have a chance to put air in it?"

His response: "No, I'll get to it today."

The next morning, you notice the same thing, but you've mentioned it twice, so you let it go. It's his car, his consequences.

The next afternoon, you get a call. "Uh, dear, my tire's gone totally flat. I don't want to drive on it and mess up the rims. Would you mind bringing that flat-fixing stuff so I can drive it to the tire store?"

You agree, and shortly you arrive at his office with the flat-fixing stuff.

At this point, you have two choices.

One choice is: *You have to tell him you were right.*

The other choice is: *Be kind.*

Stop and consider. Doesn't he already know that he messed up? Of course he does. There's no need to say, "I told you so." Besides, it will be a big ol' push, and you will probably spend the evening bickering. However, if you arrive with the decision to *be kind*, the outcome will be different. A simple "Here you go. Glad I could help" will get the tire replaced and, more than likely, lead to the kind of evening that rates an—imagine a French accent here—*oooh la la*.

As you do your internal, personal work, avoid judgmental words, and become more descriptive and kind, I wish you many *oooh la la* evenings.

KEY TEN

Great Problem Solving

(I'd like a sunny, tropical beach, thank you.)

Remember the lies that fairy tales tell? Getting married doesn't mean living happily ever after. There will be differences between spouses and problems that you'll need to solve. Every relationship has them. The trick is in how to solve them because no one is born knowing how to do this. It is an acquired skill, like riding a bike. And like learning to ride a bike, there are steps that need to be mastered in a specific order so that the skill can be acquired.

The **seven steps** to problem-solving mastery are:

➤ **Check your mindset.**

➤ **Define the problem, using descriptive terms.**

➤ **Aim for collaboration, not compromise.**

➤ **Brainstorm possible solutions.**

➤ **Evaluate the possible solutions, and select one.**

➤ **Do it.**

➤ **Follow up the solution.**

Step One: Check Your Mind-set

Before handling any problem, quickly review your automatic assumptions. Are you assuming that you have the right answer? Are you assuming that it's the other person's fault? Are you assuming that nothing will ever change? Making these types of negative assumptions is the same as using *have to*, *can't*, or *should*. You're closing down options before you've even begun the problem-solving discussion. Consider changing your mind-set to something along the lines of: "We can solve any problem together," or "It's not us against each other; it's us against this problem." This type of mind-set is amazingly successful at helping to start things off right and keep them positive. Believing that "together we can solve anything" will help you with problems both big and small.

Step Two: Define the Problem, Using Descriptive Terms

As I'm sure you've heard before, the number-one topic most couples fight about is money. But it's not really about money. It's who gets to say how you spend it. It can be about power and control. So, to stop a cycle of push/push back, consider what it is you really want, in terms of action, and find out what your partner wants. Like this:

You: I'd really like to have $50 a month for my Starbucks visits in our budget.

Partner: And I'd like to have $100 a month for green fees, so I can golf.

You: Great. Let's look at where we're spending our money and see what we can do to get green fees and Starbucks into our budget.

Step Three: Aim for Collaboration, Not Compromise

We are taught to compromise in a marriage, but what brings the greatest win-win is actually collaboration. I highly recommend reading William Ury and Roger Fisher's book, *Getting to Yes: Negotiating Agreement without*

Giving In. This book helped me understand the difference between compromising and collaborating.

The trouble with compromise is the mindset it creates. In compromise, one person takes a position: I want to go on vacation to Hawaii. The other person takes a different position: I want to go to San Diego. Each then locks in to his or her position and starts defending it.

It's automatic to start defending a position once we've taken it. I've done that myself, even when, on some level, I knew that it wasn't a great idea that I was defending. Boy, was that embarrassing.

When partners are positional, they continue to push and push back until one of them gives in enough that the other person is happy. Therefore, whoever gives up the least, wins. And boy oh boy, does this set up some negative stuff: "We did what you wanted last time. Now it's my turn." Or "Let's just split the difference." But no one's really happy.

For an extreme example of partners being positional:

Partner One: I want to vacation at a beach in Florida.

Partner Two: I want to vacation at a beach in California.

They compromise by "splitting the difference"— they vacation in Kansas, amid the amber waves of grain. Neither is happy.

Instead of this nonsense, partners need to collaborate, which means finding a solution where everyone comes

Terry Turner

out feeling like a winner. This means looking for the "underlying interests." This is a term used by Ury and Fisher. It means seeking to understand what the other person really wants by asking the questions *why* and *what*.

Partner One: What is it about Florida that you like?

Partner Two: I'd like to spend time on a sunny, tropical beach.

Now, is Florida the only place where there are sunny, tropical beaches? Of course not. If, however, there is something specific about Florida that she wanted to visit (the oldest city, St. Augustine, or the night life in Miami, etc.), you might choose to go along with her wishes and go to Florida. Remember to have a great time, which earns you "good marriage" points. But if you are looking for sunny, tropical beaches, you won't even think of looking at other places if you lock yourself in to the California-or-Florida battle. There could be an amazing bargain taking you to visit the sunny beaches in Fiji, and you'd never even notice.

As you talk with your partner about what you each want in a vacation, new home, or budget, you'll get good information about what would make you both feel as if you have a achieved a win-win.

Again, though, using the vacation example, as you talk, you may discover that your partner wants to go to Scotland, for example, because her family comes from

Scotland. Then Scotland would be the one and only place to do that. A loving spouse will accommodate his partner if possible and make plans to go to Scotland (or at least arrange for the other to go).

Most of the time, though, once you start looking for the underlying interests, there is not one and only one option. There are dozens, if not hundreds, of possible answers. That's when you can become very creative at meeting both your desires.

Step Four: Brainstorm Possible Solutions

This is where you get to practice expressing *no judgment*. Brainstorming means entertaining any idea as a possible solution. Why is *no judgment* so important? It's a right brain/left brain thing. The right hemisphere of the brain is the creative, innovative side that will come up with amazing possibilities and solutions. The left hemisphere is the analytical, logical part of the brain that analyzes things by saying, *This will work* or *this won't work*.

When we brainstorm, we are asking the right hemisphere to be creative and think of possible solutions. But if we start to analyze or critique the ideas in any way, the left hemisphere kicks in and takes over. The right hemisphere says, *Oh, you didn't really want to be creative*, and shuts off.

Here's a dialogue to demonstrate:

Partner: Where would you like to go to dinner? Joe's Grill?

You: I like Joe's, but there is always a long line.

Partner: Okay, how about Donnie's Bakery?

You: They don't have salads.

Partner: We could go to Marc's Bistro. They have good salads.

You: They're so expensive.

Does your partner feel like continuing the conversation? Probably not. That's what happens to the right brain when you start to critique options while brainstorming. The right brain stops delivering creative solutions because the left brain has taken over. A way around this—because the left brain wants to be heard as well—is to set a timer for how long to brainstorm. When the timer goes off, you can move to step five and look at what you think will work for the particular problem before you.

Step Five: Evaluate the Possible Solutions, and Select One

This is the part where you may need to do a bit of research to gather information. For example, if you're choosing where to vacation, you'd check which destination best meets each partner's needs as you've identified them in steps two and three. When you've examined all the alternatives, you select the one that looks the best to both of you. Both of you must be willing to try out the solution you've agreed upon. Agree on any money involved and who does what. The chosen solution does not have to be either partner's first choice, but both of you have to be willing to live with it.

Step Six: Do It

This is where you put your solution into action, doing what you've both agreed on in step five.

Step Seven: Follow Up the Solution

Follow-up is a crucial step that is often ignored, to the detriment of the people involved. When resolving an issue, it is essential to set a date for a follow-up discussion. It's obvious when you think about it: You cannot know whether a solution is going to work until you've tried it.

Looking at the vacation example will demonstrate how following up can be very successful. Let's say you chose to go on a cruise to Mexico. Setting a follow-up meeting means that while you are on the vacation, you look for what you like, what you don't like, and what you want to remember for next time. This prevents that grumpiness when something goes wrong or comments like "this was your idea." Instead, you could say, "Let's remember next time that we don't like this." As you plan your next vacation, remember to look for more of what you like and avoid what you don't like.

Let's say that you are on that cruise to Mexico and you discover that, to go to the shows, you have to go through the casino, where people are smoking. If you are highly allergic to cigarette smoke, you've just learned something for the follow-up. You will need to check for nonsmoking cruises or check where the shows are held in relation to smoking areas. See the difference in attitude? This small change can make you a lot more fun as a vacation partner. And keeping follow-up in your brain helps you create an even better vacation the next time.

Follow-up is even more important when setting up a family budget. What many of us do is make a budget and then that's it. It's our budget, forever and ever. Amen. If there is no follow-up and we feel locked in to the budget as it is, what happens as time passes? We might become irritated with our partner and the budget. One partner might make comments like "I don't like this" or "Wait, there's no money for green fees?" It could escalate into comments like "This was your idea," "I hate budgets," "I'm not using this budget," or even, "Budgets are stupid."

Instead, follow-up sounds like this: "Okay, here's our budget. Let's try it for a month. At the end of the month, let's look at what we like and what we don't, what's working and what we need to change." Hear the difference in word choice and attitude? You've signaled each other, and your brains, that you're staying in creative problem-solving mode.

As the month passes, you and your partner have thoughts like this: "Hmm. I need money for green fees." "I need some Starbucks money."

Then comes the end of month conversation:

Partner One: Let's look at what we can adjust to give us more money for green fees and Starbucks.

Partner Two: I'm thinking that, if we wore warmer clothes, we could turn the heat off until evening. That should save us about $100 next month. If you want to try it, we can see how it went at the end of the month.

You are checking what is possible, making adjustments, and setting a new follow-up date. Follow-up keeps the conversation going and open and keeps you engaged in problem solving.

So that's it. Those are the seven steps. It's all in how you solve your problems. Using these steps leads you to a much brighter outcome. Remember the mantra: Together, we can solve anything.

KEY ELEVEN

Match Your Partner's Mode

(I see it, I hear it, I feel it.)

Now for a subtle and profound key to use when you are having complex conversations. Be sure you use the correct *mode* when talking to your friend, partner, etc. What does that mean? Each person's brain has preferences for how they like to take in information. There are three main *modes* to remember: visual, auditory, and kinesthetic.

Imagine that you are getting directions to a place you have never been:

If you are visual, you learn and understand by seeing things. When you are trying to understand travel directions, for example, you need to have it written down. Landmarks are helpful because you can see them.

If you are auditory, you learn and understand by hearing things. If someone tells you how to get there, you will understand and remember because you heard it.

If you are kinesthetic, you learn and understand by doing things. You mentally drive the map as you receive the directions. Once you've driven there, you can always get there again.

Now it's your turn. If you've bought something that needs assembly, do you read the instructions, have them read to you, or just start assembling? If you're visual and your partner is auditory, you might read the instructions aloud so you can see them and your partner can hear them. If you are kinesthetic, you may simply ignore the instructions and start assembling.

How does this apply when problem solving? Let me give another personal example: Early in my marriage, I was talking about a problem to my husband. Since I'm visual, I was making eye contact. Since I'm also kinesthetic, I was also gesturing. He said, "When you look directly at me and gesture while you talk, I feel attacked." Wow. That was helpful to know.

As I processed what he said, I realized that he was very auditory. He took in so much information just from the nuances in my voice that my face-to-face position and my gesturing created an overload. From that day on, whenever we had important conversations, I would sit beside him and sometimes even dim the lights. Of course, because I'm visual, I'd be glancing at his face to see what his responses were. Because I was using his *mode*, the problem solving was easier. As we use the mode most comfortable for the other person, we become much more effective in our communication. We can request that other people use our mode when they are relaying information important to us.

Is there a sure-fire way to tell which mode or combination of modes you are? Yes. Become aware of your eye movements.

If you look to the left, that's *recall*; to the right is *construction*; to the center is *synthesis*. An important thing to remember about construction is that a person who does this is not necessarily lying as they say on TV. The person looking to the right could also be carefully wording his next sentence, trying to be descriptive instead of judgmental, or trying to word it tactfully.

Scientists have discovered that if you are accessing the visual part of your brain, your eyes will look up, left, right, or center, and you'll be looking toward the ceiling. If you are accessing the auditory part of your brain, your eyes look horizontally left, right, or center. If you are accessing the kinesthetic part of your brain, your eyes look down toward the floor, left, right or center.

Try it. Vividly imagine your favorite vacation spot. Where did your eyes go? Now, vividly imagine walking in your front door. Where did your eyes go? Now imagine the face of someone you love. This is fun, isn't it? Subtly start noticing the eye movements of the people in your life. You don't want to be obvious or "in their face" about this, of course. In addition, notice the words they use. "I get the picture" would be a visual person. "That rings a bell"— auditory. "I have a handle on it" would be kinesthetic.

A person who is visual needs to be able to see things, either in a physical picture or word pictures. If the person is auditory, too much visual input is probably a distraction.

The tone of the conversation itself is also important. A very auditory person may even prefer problem solving while talking on the phone with you rather than talking in person. A kinesthetic person enjoys movement and action. Walking while talking over a problem is useful to the kinesthetic person.

Below are a few more examples of what different modes enjoy.

Auditory
Loves books on tape
Likes being told you care
Likes conversation and music

Kinesthetic
Likes receiving a hug
Likes to walk or move when on the phone
Enjoys food with textures, finger foods

Visual
Likes beautiful table settings at dinner
Likes reading books
Likes receiving cards and letters

Some things will cover more than one mode. Cards with music for example, meet the modes of both visual and auditory. Flowers are visual and kinesthetic. A roaring fire is visual, auditory, and kinesthetic.

When you match the mode of the other person, you improve her ability to comprehend and remember what you are saying. As you communicate with your friends, partner, etc., by using their preferred modes of interaction, you will notice that you are getting through more easily and more effectively.

KEY TWELVE

Defuse or Eliminate Crabs

Let's talk about crabs—please, I mean the seafood kind. Have you ever been to a fresh seafood market? If you have, you've seen the barrel of crabs. Did you notice that there is rarely a lid on the barrel, yet the crabs don't escape? Do you know why? Because, as one crab starts to climb up and out, the other crabs grab him and yank him back down. I kid you not.

The sad truth is, there are a lot of crabs out there, and some of us live with them. As you work on yourself and drop some assumptions, stop playing the game of push/push back, stop "reacting mad," you'll notice that you are enjoying life more and feeling a lot happier. That's when the crabs get angry at you. The crab attitude is this: *In this family, we are all miserable. Get back to being miserable with the rest of us.* One way to protect yourself is to realize that you might be dealing with crabs. It's not about you at all. The poison they spew at others is only information about how painful their lives are right now and how much they want to share their hurt by dumping on you.

I suggest **three techniques** for dealing with crabs who criticize you:

➢ **Remember to stay calm.**
➢ **Agree with any truth.**
➢ **Find out what's really going on.**

Remember to Stay Calm

The first thing to do if you are dealing with someone who is being a crab is stay calm and remember: $E + T = F = R = O$. If you "react mad," you are rewarding the crab and he will keep pinching at you.

One way I stay calm is to remind myself that people can only give out what they have inside. I tell myself, *Maybe he's having a terrible day and wants to share it with me.* No, thank you.

A quick reminder, as we saw in $E + T = F = R = O$: it's not what the person says, it's what we think about it that causes our feelings.

Spend some time getting in touch with your own personal strategies to keep calm. You can mentally put yourself in a place you enjoy, like a beach in Hawaii or snowboarding in the mountains. One of my favorites is to tell myself, *Wow, I can see "crab" tattooed across her forehead. Nice colors.* Or you can remember to breathe, count to ten, and so on. I encourage you to discover and use whatever strategies work for you.

Another important aspect of remaining calm is being aware of our nonverbal communication. It's crucial.

Why? Because, if we are broadcasting our anger through tight fists and scrunched faces, any calm words that come out of our mouths will be meaningless.

Humans are hard-wired to notice all the micro-expressions in a person's face and body language. It's one of our survival mechanisms as a species. Being able to tell if an enemy is about to attack or is simply checking us out proved very useful to our ancestors, so it got passed down to future generations.

If my tone of voice is sarcastic or nasty or my face and body are tightly clenched, I am sending an "attack" message nonverbally. What's the problem with that? If I send one message with my words and a different message with my nonverbal (voice and body signals), people will believe my tone of voice and body. The nonverbal message trumps what I actually say.

What if a friend has told you in the past that you are very important to her, but, over the course of two weeks, you've left several messages on her voice mail asking for help, and you've gotten no response. You e-mail three times and still don't hear back. You know from mutual friends that she is not out of town, crazy busy at work, or dealing with a crisis. What do you believe about your importance to this person? You believe that you are not important. You believe the nonverbal message.

People believe actions much more than they believe words.

What if your sweetie says that he is not angry at you, but his face is bright red, his jaw is tight, and he is holding his arms against his sides with his fists clenched? Yep. You believe your sweetie's body, not his words—and he is steaming mad.

These examples illustrate why we need to pay attention to our own nonverbal messages, especially when we are dealing with a crab. Any nonverbal "angry" is a reaction. If we react, we "reward" the crabs for trying to yank us back down.

Once you have accessed your mental calm, you can move to the next part of this key.

Agree with Any Truth

Let's move to "agree with any truth" by taking a look at some common conversations between friends and/or spouses. Perhaps you too have heard or participated in dialogues like these.

Mary says in a snippy tone of voice, "That dress is really red."

Susan says, "No, it's not." (And off they go into a game of push/push back—yes it is, no it's not.)

Or:

Susan apologizes: "Oh, no. It's too red. I look ugly."

Another familiar example:

Jenifer: You didn't put the dishes in the dishwasher.

Carl: It's your turn. I did them yesterday.

Or:

Carl: Yeah, yeah, yeah, I'll do them. (And they don't get done.)

Or:

Hayley: You're not very thoughtful.

Mark might say, "Yes, I am" or "Neither are you" or mumble and grumble as he walks away.

I call these kinds of interactions attack and react as well as push/push back. It goes downhill from there, with anger and resentment building up, creating a whole list of "things I'm still mad at you about."

When you stop reacting to someone's crabby criticism, when you no longer get upset or push back, she will try a little harder to see if she can get you upset. When you continue to stay calm and you either agree with any truth or find out what's really going on, you will no longer be free entertainment. The crab will go off and find someone else to pick on. Hurray!

I know this may sound crazy, but often in criticism, there will be a thread of truth. You need to put on your detective hat to find it, because it may take some work to discover it buried in the hurtful phrase. Why is this important? By finding the thread of truth and working with it, you defuse the criticism. You have not engaged in a game of push/push back.

There are two main ways to work with the thread of truth:

- Acknowledge what is accurate in the criticism.
- Play a game of basic logic.

When you acknowledge what is accurate, the crab has thrown a rock—but you have moved the can. When you follow the logic to its conclusion, you have turned yourself into fog.

How can you move the can off the fence? When someone criticizes you, quickly analyze what was said and consider whether any part of the criticism could be true. If you find and agree with a truth, the rock the person has thrown has no can to hit.

Going back to the red dress example from above, you would seek out the truth—you are wearing a red dress—and respond this way:

Mary (in a snippy tone of voice): That dress is really red.

Susan (in a calm and happy tone of voice because she likes her dress): It really is. It is just so red.

Mary: Yeah. It is. (And off Mary goes to find someone else to pick on because you won't play.)

Or:

Jenifer (in an accusatory tone): You didn't put the dishes in the dishwasher, and you said you would.

Carl (calm and penitent): Oh, my gosh, you're right. I didn't. I'm sorry. I need to pay better attention to that. I'll go do them right now. (He then goes and does them.)

It's fairly straightforward. Before pushing back, pause and examine the truth you have discovered in the criticism.

For an example of the game of logic, imagine that your younger brother has questioned your math abilities by stating you are not very good at math. You feel insecure about your math abilities. It's tempting to push back. Instead, ask yourself, *Am I better at math than I was when I was born?*

Yes.

If you keep working at it, will you continue to improve?

Yes.

That's the way it works. The truth is you *could* be better—notice I'm not saying you need to be or that you believe you need to improve your math skills, only that theoretically, you could be better. You can truthfully respond, "I could be better."

My bet is, your younger brother will respond with something like, "Uh. Sure. Yeah … that's what I said."

He will go off to seek someone else to throw rocks at because you just turned into fog, and he didn't see it coming.

Find Out What's Really Going On

Depending upon the critical comment aimed at you, you can either choose to agree with any truth or find out what's really going on.

By gathering more information, you will discover if the critic is simply being a crab or trying to be helpful but lacking in communication skills. (If so, feel free to buy him a copy of this book.)

This method examines the truth from a different angle. You'll learn to engage in the conversation in a different way by delving deeper into the other person's motives. Asking questions about the criticism will lead you to discover what is really happening. Is the critic sharing something useful that you need to know? Is he asking for a behavior change? Does he simply have very poor communication skills? Is he simply throwing rocks? The way to find out is to *ask*. What a concept.

Here are some sample dialogues to show you how to do this:

Hayley: You're not very thoughtful.

Mark: Wow. Well, that's certainly not who I want to be. What am I doing that's not thoughtful?

Try to remain calm and speak in a level voice. Otherwise you have reacted overtly, and every time that crab wants some fun, she'll think of you to pick on.

At this point, Hayley, if she's being a crab that day, might respond, "You should know" or "I can't think of an example right now."

A good response to that is, "Please, the next time I do something that isn't thoughtful, let me know immediately so I can address it."

Hayley will feel that you've heard her concerns and the conversation is now over. The funny part of this is that you'll probably never hear about it again. It was just her version of "I'm having a bad day and wanted to share it with you."

Sometimes, though, Hayley may share with Mark something that he's doing that's not thoughtful. Mark can thank her for telling him and quit doing it. No stress. No big drama.

What if Hayley's not being a crab but says, "It was my birthday yesterday. You didn't even send me a card."

Ouch. Not pleasant to hear, but okay, it's good to know that she is upset that you forgot. At that point, you agree with the truth: "Oh, my gosh. I can't believe I forgot your birthday. I am so sorry."

Then make a plan to make up for it: "Let's go out to dinner Saturday for a belated celebration." Or "I'm putting a reminder in my calendar right now for next year. You'll be getting a card early." If you want to add a wonderful extra, go hunt up a belated birthday card and get it in the mail. Immediately. Spending time doing something like buying a belated card will give Hayley concrete proof that she is important to you.

If you're tired of playing push/push back, remember to agree with any truth and find out what's really going on.

One final example, a true story:

Early in my career, a young man came up after class and said to me, "You're not a very good teacher."

Ouch. At that point, all my self-doubts about my teaching ability were vividly displayed on my internal monitor, and I started mentally reviewing all the ways I thought I wasn't a good teacher. Happily, in the next second, I remembered, *I teach this stuff. I could use it.* I decided to find out what was really going on.

I calmly replied, "That's not good. What is it about my teaching you don't like?"

His response: "Women should wear high heels."

I swear to goodness this is true. At this point, my biggest challenge was to keep a straight face. Because it was a communication class where I also talk about interview clothes, I confirmed that when I do workshops in the community, I don't wear flats or tennis shoes. I'm in a suit and heels, because that nonverbal message is crucial. I also told him how glad I was that even though it was unorthodox, the college allowed me to wear tennis shoes because of a problem I have with my arches. He nodded and smiled, because he knew I had heard his concerns and addressed them.

Then I double-checked. "Is there anything else about my teaching you don't like?"

He said, "No, that was it. Women should wear high heels."

I smiled and replied, "Thanks for sharing that. Have a great day." He thanked me and went on his way. I went on mine.

Now, because I am human, later I told my dog about the strange experience. At the same time, I loved it, because it demonstrated to me how crazy we can get by what we think someone might mean by what he or she is saying. Then when we hear what the person is actually thinking, sometimes the biggest challenge is not to laugh in surprise. Remembering this can be a great way to reduce the stress in your life, and it can also be the beginning of an easier time in problem solving.

Stay calm, agree with any truth, and find out what's really going on.

Marking Your Success

As you begin to incorporate the twelve keys into your relationships, you might find it difficult. It is reassuring to know that the *this is hard* feeling is a positive step on the road to change. In fact, by reading this book, you are already starting the process of change. You are becoming aware of your good or bad habits of communication.

You can't change something unless you know that you are doing it. So, hearing yourself using the word *but* is fantastic. You are paying attention, which is the beginning of changing yourself for the better. Yay!

The process goes like this:

Clueless

To explain this process, I'm going to use the "reduce your *but*" key. At this step, you don't realize the effect of your saying "but," and you're wondering why people get so irritated when you give them feedback.

You are in the clueless step. You don't even know what you don't know. You aren't paying attention, and you have no knowledge of the need to change or the way to do it.

Here are some examples to explain what I mean. When my granddaughter was four, she was convinced that if she could just put my car in gear, she would be able to drive my car. She didn't even know what she didn't know about driving—those minor details such as, it really helps if you are tall enough to see out of the windshield—and able to reach the brake, too. We always supervised her when she was near my car, especially if she had snagged the car keys. I remain grateful to whoever designed my car so that it can't be put into gear without the brake pedal depressed because my granddaughter firmly believed if she could just get the car into gear, she could drive.

Let's talk about driving a stick shift. Same principles apply. Imagine that you are about six years old and you watch your dad smoothly shift gears. You think, *That's easy. I could do that.* You don't even know what you don't know.

As a last example: Have you ever met someone with lousy communication skills? And the person wonders why he has no friends? Yep, that person is right there at the first step. She doesn't even know what she doesn't know. I suspect that some crabs live at this step forever.

This Is Hard

Okay, you've begun to learn the new skills, such as reducing your *but*. You realize that you use the word *but* all the time. Unfortunately, you might mentally start beating yourself up, saying, *Oh, no. I'm terrible at this.* You might even give up on changing by saying, *This is too hard.*

Instead, this is where you need to give yourself huge amounts of credit for moving out of "clueless" and into "this is hard." You can tell yourself (remember self-fulfilling prophecies), *I use the word* but *right now. I'm going to learn to use* and *instead.*

Once you realize that you do something that isn't working, you are well on the way to making a positive change and mastering new skills. So at this stage, you hear the "but" right after it comes out of your mouth. Whoops. Then, at this point, you quickly correct yourself. It's a very awkward stage. It's similar to how you probably felt the first few times you were behind the wheel of a car as a teenager. You might have told yourself, *This is hard. There is so much to remember. I'm still willing to learn it.*

Just for fun, think back to something you didn't know you were going to have to learn about driving. Something that was hard. How about how firmly you had to press the brake so you stopped in a timely manner but didn't make everyone in the car get whiplash? For me, it was how to keep the car centered in my lane on the highway when the wind off the ocean was really strong. Yet because you were motivated to learn how to drive, you just kept working on it.

Getting Better and Better

You have mastered reducing your *but*. You pay a lot of attention to doing it correctly. You catch the "but" just before it comes out of your mouth and rework it. Way to go. You have it down. You are aware that you still have to pay a lot of attention to getting it said without that "but."

How about another driving example? Imagine that you have learned the skills of driving a stick shift. As you are driving, you've not quite crested a steep hill when the light changes to red. You're stopped on the hill, facing up. What are you thinking while you wait for the green light? Yes. Your entire focus is on what you have to do when the light goes green so you don't roll backward or stall. You're hoping you don't mess up. You are paying intense, constant attention to using your new skills correctly.

If you keep using any new skill and work at improving it, you will get better. You will no longer have to pay special attention to shifting gears except in special circumstances. It works just like that with all your communication skills.

It's a Part of You

You have arrived. The skills have become so much a part of you that only in extreme circumstances (trauma, no sleep, etc.) do you need to pay close attention. You have completely integrated the skill. You rarely even think a "but" sentence unless you're deliberately using it in an example. You use "and" instead. This is the final step in the process of learning a new skill.

This is the place you will be after a bit of time and effort of practicing your new skills. It will be so good. The more you use your new skills, the better you'll be at communicating effectively.

Watch how the others in your life respond to your new skills. It makes the time and effort you spent learning them worthwhile, doesn't it?

Get Out There and Do It

I'd like to close with one last bit of encouragement to start using your new communication skills by sharing a story about my granddaughter.

My granddaughter, Natie, is an inspiration for me. In fact, she came up with an alternate title for this book—*How to be Happier and Kinder by Treating Other People Better.* I loved it.

Also, she recently reminded me of a great life motto I'd like to share—*feel the fear and do it anyway* (thank you, Susan Jeffers).

Her first-grade class was putting on a musical version of the *Three Little Pigs* story. Natie has a lovely voice, and she'd been selected to play the role of Mama Pig, which meant she had a solo—the first solo of the program. She had to walk out on stage, jiggling her tushy to accent her pig-tail, circle her three little pig-children, walk to center stage, and sing her solo. She was desperately nervous about this. In fact, each time I saw the teacher in the weeks before the performance, she asked me to encourage Natie to sing out, since she was singing too softly to be heard.

Natie and I started talking about stage fright and performance anxiety, how being scared is an expression of the fight or flight syndrome, how many famous people actually get stage fright too. I shared with her that I've had it on several occasions. Hey, I present lectures as a living; you think I haven't had stage fright? Natie was still nervous, still singing as if she was in a church.

Then, I talked to a wonderful colleague who is a professor of vocal music. I asked if she thought I should sign Natie up for voice lessons. Liz gave me the key: Natie didn't need voice lessons at this time in her life. She just needed to believe that she could sing louder.

I shifted gears and started providing support instead of discussions. When Natie mentioned how scared she was, I agreed it was scary to get up on stage and sing a solo. I said that the fear could grip her, but she was in charge of her thoughts and feelings. I reminded her how her family and everyone in the audience would be supporting all the children and enjoying every minute of the performance— her solo included. We were all proud of the children for taking the risk to perform, and we knew she could do her solo loud enough for everyone to hear.

And oh, my goodness. The performance arrived, and Natie rocked it. She walked out with a piggy-tail swish to remember, opened up her heart, and sang—no microphone needed. She had found her stage presence.

So now, when I'm worried about learning a new skill, I remember Natie's Mama Pig—and I just get out there, swish my tail, and sing.

And on that note, I ask you to imagine a world of people who enjoy their lives, care for and uplift each other, and encourage success—and do it all through better communication skills. And with your new skills, you too can become a part of it.

Printed in the United States
By Bookmasters